**P**eter Maggs grew up in Ealing in west London. He left school with one 'O' level and spent several years playing rock 'n' roll with various bands. After a spell of conventional work and night school, he studied Physics at university, and followed a career in the engineering industry. He developed an interest in nineteenth-century social history through investigations into the genealogy of his family, and took early retirement to spend more time doing research. *Reverend Duke and the Amesbury Oliver* is his fourth book. He has also contributed articles, mainly on genealogy, to various magazines.

# Reverend Duke and the Amesbury Oliver

Peter Maggs

Published by Mirli Books 2020

Published in the UK by
Mirli Books
21 Highfield Road
Chelmsford CM1 2NF

ISBN 978-0-9562870-4-5

A catalogue record for this book
is available from the British Library

Also by Peter Maggs:
*Henry's Trials*
*Smethurst's Luck*
*Murder in the Red Barn*

Design: Gill England
Print: MBC Print Consultancy

This book is dedicated to the memory of my father, Norman Ernest Maggs. He discovered the previously unknown, secret investigation into the death of fifteen-year-old George Wheeler in the files at the Public Record Office, and christened him *The Amesbury Oliver*.

*People are a problem.*

Douglas Adams,
*The Hitchhiker's Guide to the Galaxy*

# Acknowledgements

Grateful thanks are due, as ever, to staff at the British Library, Kings Cross, The National Archives at Kew, and The Wiltshire and Swindon History Centre, Chippenham. I am particularly grateful to Sandy Haynes and the Wiltshire Museum, Devizes, for the generous provision of some unpublished transcripts of letters between Sir Richard Colt Hoare and William Cunnington; also to John Sims for pointing out the discrepancy in George Wheeler's age and researching details of the Wheeler family, and Roger Jones for reading the manuscript and making a number of helpful suggestions.

Once more I have to thank Diane Hardy for her superlative attention to detail in proofreading the draft text, and my wife Jacky, who is my final arbiter in questions of style, spelling and grammar.

**Errata**

Page 4, paragraph 2, line 19, delete 'nine', insert 'eight'.

Pages 158 & 168. The analysis confuses John Pothecary, Mr Duke's witness who came into the room shortly *after* the incident between Ralfs and George Wheeler, with Abraham Joules, who *was* an eyewitness and was present during the incident, but had *not* been interviewed by Duke beforehand; he was called by the enquiry chairman.

Page 205, add to references: *Wiltshire and its Worthies*, Joseph Stratford, Salisbury Brown, 1882.

Details of books and articles written by Peter Maggs can be found at www.mirlibooks.com

# Contents

## Notes on the Text

The correspondence between various members of the Amesbury Union and the Poor Law Commissioners provides the bulk of reference material used in the construction of this history. Much of the letter writing was initiated by Edward Duke, and in order to understand his frequent questions and comments, as well as the actions of his brother guardians and responses from the Poor Law Commissioners, it is helpful to be familiar with both the old and the new Poor Laws. The main period concerned in this narrative, roughly ten years between 1834 and 1844, was one of transition from laws dating from the reign of Elizabeth I, to the requirements of the 1834 Act. Poor Law unions and union workhouses were not introduced by the new Act, but they became effectively mandatory as a result of it, and the contentious 'outdoor relief' was henceforth largely, but not entirely, removed. Questions of how to deal with individual cases of need before the new union workhouses were ready for occupation generated much correspondence. Furthermore, the subsequent day-to-day operation of the new workhouse at Amesbury exercised Reverend Duke considerably, and this was responsible for the majority of the documents in the commissioners' files.

A review of the Poor Laws is contained in Appendix 1. The source for most of this information is the work by Beatrice and Sydney Webb, published in 1929. Mention should also be made of Peter Higginbotham's excellent website, *The Workhouse*, which summarizes the progress of the Poor Laws from the fourteenth century, and contains copies of a number of the original Acts of Parliament.

One observation, made more in mitigation of mistakes made by this author than anything else, is that the primary source of information used for this work, the correspondence in the files of the Poor Law Commissioners, is all handwritten. Until the advent of the typewriter, all correspondence, notes etc. had to be recorded in this way. Government, commerce, and other bureaucracies employed a positive army of clerks. Their sole occupation was to write letters and memoranda, read incoming letters, and make copies of all for the files. And here I cannot resist quoting from George Eliot's *Middlemarch*. Fred Vincey, a well-meaning but rather aimless young man who had failed initially to take his university degree, is being taken in hand by his future father-in-law as regards the farm management business. He has been asked to copy some lines to assess his handwriting:

> At that time [the 1830s] the opinion existed that it was beneath a gentleman to write legibly, or with a hand in the least suitable to a clerk. Fred wrote the lines demanded in a hand as gentlemanly as that of any viscount or bishop of the day: the vowels were all alike and the consonants only distinguishable as turning up or down, the strokes had a blotted solidity and the letters disdained to keep the line— in short, it was a manuscript of that venerable kind easy to interpret when you know beforehand what the writer means.

The written correspondence on which the present account is based falls perfectly into Eliot's description. Occasionally there is some beautiful cursive copperplate, always marked 'copy', where a clerk had made a copy of a document for filing. Mostly though, letters from Mr Duke, draft letters from the Poor Law Commissioners—those were the file copies, the originals having been sent to the addressee—and particularly written material from Henry Walter Parker, the Assistant Poor Law Commissioner, are 'as gentlemanly as that of any viscount or bishop'. It is interesting to speculate how much time and effort must have been expended in those times just attempting to read some of the scrawl that passed for official documents, and how many mistakes must have been made when important communications were virtually illegible. In my researches, I have encountered an instance where a clergyman spent six months in prison because his comprehensive defence statement, written as a brief for his barrister while he was on remand, could not be deciphered by a professional clerk.

The evidence given during the 1844 enquiry into the death of fifteen-year-old George Wheeler, which forms the main focus of this book, was written down by Henry Parker as it was presented; his handwriting was at least as bad as any that I have encountered in this investigation. As will be explained in the introduction, my father first discovered Parker's written evidence in the early 1960s. My mother, Annemarie Maggs, working as a shorthand typist, was well versed in reading 'difficult' handwriting. She was able to make a partial transcription from photocopies. This was limited just to that relating directly to George Wheeler and amounted to only thirty per cent of the testimony given. It excluded details of three other charges made by Mr Duke, as well as the considerable evidence given as to the character of the workhouse master and his wife. But in deciphering the quirks of Mr Parker's handwriting and his occasional use of shorthand symbols, my mother provided me with a veritable 'Rosetta Stone' that allowed the rest of the evidence to be transcribed. If any errors have crept into that transcription, either by her or me, then Mr Parker's execrable handwriting must be the primary offender.

The major source of reference material used in this narrative is the extensive correspondence between Mr Duke, the Poor Law Commissioners, and Richard Wilson, the clerk to the Amesbury Union. There are also letters from Henry Walker Parker and Rev Gorges Lowther, the chairman of the guardians at Amesbury. It is tempting, therefore, to quote extensively from this correspondence in order that authenticity and the feel of the period is invoked. This practice can detract from the narrative flow, and therefore I have attempted to limit the reproduction of large amounts of quoted material wherever possible. There are, nevertheless, numerous instances where I have judged that a summary or paraphrase of what was said would lose authority or accuracy. A bibliography, a selective index, and a list of references are provided, and virtually all material is in the public domain.

Edward Duke was referred to in the source material as 'The Rev. Edward Duke', 'The Rev. Mr Duke', or just 'Mr Duke', together with one or two other variants. In order to streamline the narrative, he will usually be written as 'Mr Duke'. The head of a union workhouse, appointed by and reporting to the board of guardians, was designated 'The Master' by the new Poor Law Act, and that term is used in this narrative. However, in the correspondence between the Amesbury Union, the Poor Law Commissioners, and Mr Duke, and most particularly in much of the evidence presented to the 1844 enquiry, the master was referred to frequently and interchangeably as 'The Governor'. This usage may have arisen as a result of the paupers' habit of referring to him by that title. When directly quoting from sources, the text will follow whichever term is being used.

One final comment on layout. If this history of Mr Duke's activities were a proper biography, the events would be recorded more or less in the order in which they occurred. His labours can be separated into three broad categories: literary and antiquarian works, duty as a JP, and service as an ex officio guardian of the Amesbury Union. Although Mr Duke owed his status as a guardian to the fact that he was a magistrate, for the most part there was little interaction between the two. He commenced his magistracy in 1816, but it was during the period 1828 to 1839 that he mainly courted controversy on the bench. The term of his Poor Law Guardianship was from 1835 to 1844, and Mr Duke's antiquarian and literary activities occurred in fits and starts throughout the period between

1806 and 1849. In order to preserve the flow and maintain continuity in the narrative, Mr Duke's time on the bench will be covered in one chapter, and his Poor Law Guardianship in two more. His literary and antiquarian efforts, even though they continued over a period of more than 40 years, from before he became a magistrate until well after he finished his association with both the bench and the Amesbury Union, will occupy a further single chapter. A strict chronological sequence of events where the narrative switches between quite different activities would, in my view, be far less satisfactory than the method I have adopted. Whether this works or not, the reader must judge.

# Introduction

When I was quite young, I remember accompanying my father to Somerset House where he wanted to consult the national indexes for births, marriages, and deaths. To show me how the system worked, we looked up my own birth, which had been listed in September 1945. Father had become interested in the genealogy of his family, and had come in search of the record of one or other of his forebears. I recall a room full of great tomes ranged on shelves, some in galleries with wrought-iron railings.

The process of locating a record was relatively straightforward. When a range of years for the search had been determined, the large and heavy volumes covering that period, four to a year, had to be taken from the shelves and searched alphabetically for the record, using special inclined desks designed for the purpose. Even then, only a name, date, and registration district could be found, but these enabled a copy of the appropriate certificate to be purchased from the General Register Office. These centralized records had commenced only in July 1837, so anyone wishing to look further back in time was obliged to search the many individual parish records (there were over 15,000 parishes in England and Wales), and this meant visiting the parish in question. The process was fraught; permission to view the register books had to be sought from the parish priest or one or other of the parish officers. Some were friendly and disposed to help, others were not. Some charged a fee, some just requested a contribution to the poor box. The process could be difficult and success was far from assured.

My father was particularly interested in the part of his family that had lived on Salisbury Plain in the vicinity of Stonehenge. His grandfather, Frank Maggs, son of a Wiltshire shepherd, had been born in that area, and the close association of the enigmatic stone circle with the family fascinated my father. In his eyes, Stonehenge lent a special resonance to the significance of those particular forebears. When he could spare the time and money, Father would travel to Wiltshire and, facing down the indifference or open hostility of the keepers of the parish records, would attempt to assemble the family history from the local churches of Maddington, Rollstone, Shrewton, the Orchestons, and Tilshead.

It was particularly difficult for him. My father had committed several cardinal sins in the eyes of people in the various social strata with whom he came into contact. He had had little formal education having left school at the age of thirteen, but continuing his education himself, he was widely read and able to hold an intelligent conversation at all levels of society. He had taught himself French and German to a very high standard. He could also write clear and elegant English and had, just before he left school, won an all-London essay competition organized by the RSPCA. But he was always fairly scruffily turned out, rejecting smart clothes believing, as Solzhenitsyn put it, that they 'embellish the ugly and disguise the wicked'. Thus the educated thought him a dangerous upstart, the not so educated thought him a 'smart Alec', and his unkempt appearance raised suspicion at all levels. Distant relations thought he was after their money, and the Oxbridge educated clergy no doubt suspected him of being a dangerous Communist with subversion in mind.

Nevertheless he persisted, and slowly a picture of the Wiltshire part of the family emerged. My father was able to augment this with visits to the Public Record Office in Chancery Lane where the early census records could be viewed on microfilm. These provided family groups with ages and occupations, greatly assisting in establishing who was who, and who was related to whom.

Such a process can seem to some to be a fairly sterile activity; a list of names and their relation to each other tells us nothing about what the people were like or how they lived. My father wanted to know more, and his enquiring mind led him to the records of the Amesbury Union Workhouse. He knew from the parish records, the census returns, and his grandfather's first-hand testimony, that most of his immediate Wiltshire ancestors had been either shepherds or agricultural day labourers. Their incomes would have been subject to the vagaries of the weather and fickle employers, and they would probably have been on 'short commons' for much of the time. He reasoned that there was a strong possibility that some of them had been given poor relief, and wondered whether there were records of those transactions.

The Poor Law Amendment Act of 1834 required that henceforth, relief to the destitute and infirm was to be provided through a central workhouse which served a number of parishes; twenty-three around Stonehenge had been subsumed into the Amesbury Union, with its new workhouse at Amesbury. The Public Record Office held the correspondence between the guardians of the Amesbury Union and the Poor Law Commissioners, and my father scanned the files eagerly looking for records relating to his ancestors. He was not successful; the only paupers' names appearing in the records were related to special cases where the local guardians were unable to decide how to proceed and needed guidance. He did though, find something else. He described it to me as the record of a secret trial. It concerned an enquiry to determine whether the workhouse master had cruelly ill-treated a crippled boy who had subsequently died. Around 100 pages of evidence taken over a period of four days were contained in the files.

This was potentially a most interesting discovery and eminently publishable. The trial at Amesbury had taken place in 1844, just a few years after the publication of *Oliver Twist*, and one year before the notorious scandal at the Andover Workhouse; Andover was around twelve miles from Amesbury and the adjacent union. The affair at Andover ultimately brought down the Poor Law Commissioners. Furthermore, one of the senior players caught up in the Andover scandal, Henry Walter Parker, had conducted the secret enquiry at the Amesbury Union. His perceived misconduct at Andover led to his forcible resignation as an assistant Poor Law Commissioner under very acrimonious circumstances.

An important question for my father was the form in which an account should be published. He decided to write it up as a historical novel, called *The Amesbury Oliver* after Dickens' boy hero. The book never saw the light of day. Several publishers turned it down and eventually my father lost interest, concentrating instead on factual descriptive writing on social history. Decades later and after his death, I re-read the text of his novel and the evidence transcripts, and decided to look first-hand at the source material on which he had based his account. The original files were requested from the National Archives at Kew, where all the public records had been moved after the closure of Chancery Lane, and I spent many hours poring over them. What I found was astonishing. My father had included in his book only details of the enquiry and the immediate build-up to it, but he had barely disturbed the surface of what had been a simmering cauldron of resentment. Edward Duke, the person who made the accusation against the workhouse master, was himself a guardian of the workhouse and a Wiltshire magistrate. He had spent the previous nine years criticising the Amesbury Union and its officers, of which he was one, and this was the third occasion on which there had been a formal hearing into his complaints. None of this background was mentioned in my father's account, in which Mr Duke was portrayed as a patrician, sympathetic figure, frustrated in his quest for justice for the poor.

In fact, Edward Duke was far from being sympathetic; he was a grievance-hunting, petty, and disputatious busybody, subject to fits of caprice and petulance, and not short of hubris and ego. The quirky nature of his personality illuminates his many letters and the two rather bizarre books that he paid to have published. It is quite clear from the extant correspondence, that the 1844 hearing was the culmination of an enormous amount of frustration, bitterness, and resentment on both sides which had been building up over a number of years. This was a story that just had to be told.

Apart from a few miscellaneous letters, there are three primary sources of information about Edward Duke's character and behaviour in public life. Firstly, the newspaper reports of his activities during the Wiltshire Quarter Sessions detail his participation in the debates concerning the governance of the county with his brother magistrates. Then there is the extensive correspondence, some of it very vexed, between the Amesbury Union, Edward Duke, and the Poor Law Commissioners; it is from these documents that details of the enquiry were obtained. Lastly, Mr Duke speaks to us through the letters he wrote to the *Gentleman's Magazine*, the 26-part exposition of his grand theory on Stonehenge in the *Salisbury and Wiltshire Gazette*, and his two books. The books are, in different ways, odd in the extreme. One of them, *The Druidical Temples of the County of Wilts*, has a portrait of Duke holding a book with *Stonehenge* printed on the spine. I remember quite well my father showing this picture to one of his pals at the British Museum Reading Room (the old home of the British Library) in my presence, and asking something like: 'Is that not a picture of a just man with a sense of charity and mercy?' Through Mr Duke's first book, *Prolusiones Historicae*, it is possible to deduce a sardonic personality not taking itself too seriously. Less so in the second book, where he lays forth his grand unified theory explaining the origins of Stonehenge, Silbury Hill, and Avebury. Nevertheless, in both books he portrays himself as an experienced and knowledgeable antiquary with his classical education very much on show.

There should have been a fourth primary source of information about the Amesbury Union, namely the minutes recording the proceedings of the meetings of the guardians. Those for the period 1835, when the union commenced, until 1839 are extant and deposited in the Wiltshire and Swindon History Centre, as are the minutes for 1845 and thereafter. For the period 1840 to 1844, covering the date of the alleged assault in 1840 and the build-up to the enquiry of 1844, the books containing the minutes are missing. They have not been abstracted by an overenthusiastic researcher— for a short while I even wondered whether my father might somehow have removed them. The prosaic truth is that they were never deposited in the archive. Was there a conspiracy? Did the Amesbury Guardians suppress them because of an incriminating entry? Did Mr Duke 'acquire' them, perhaps to use as evidence in an action against the union following the 1844 enquiry? It is tempting to suspect skulduggery given the turbulence of those four years in the life of the union, and adherents to the conspiracy theory of history might be satisfied with that explanation. Perhaps an enthusiastic guardian or clerk in later years borrowed the minute books with the intention of writing up the saga of Edward Duke and George Wheeler, and 'forgot' to return them. It is intriguing to speculate whether those records of the guardians' meetings would be able to throw any further light on events, and it is not impossible that they may turn up someday.

I have frequently asked myself whether this narrative is, or should be, a biography of Mr Duke. After all, much effort has been expended in searching the records for references to him and his life and works. On the bench, and with the exception of his intransigence over the removal of one of the assize courts to Devizes and an unwarranted accusation against a prison governor, Mr Duke's performance as a magistrate was unremarkable enough. But in his capacity as a Poor-Law guardian, he made the lives of virtually everyone who came into contact with him a misery. He was responsible for the dissipation of thousands of man-hours dealing with his unsupported proposals and groundless complaints, and this was time and effort which should have been used in the care of the poor. George Bernard Shaw observed:

> The reasonable man adapts himself to the world: the unreasonable one persists in trying to adapt the world to himself. Therefore all progress depends on the unreasonable man.

He might have added that progress can be overrated, and that the population of the planet might live more peaceful and contented lives without people like Edward Duke.

On reflection, although aspects of this account are probably closer to a very imperfect biography than anything else, it lacks many of the characteristics of a 'good' example of that genre; no attempt has been made to enquire into Mr Duke's personal life other than a broad outline of his immediate family. The biographical detail that it does contain, quite intentionally serves only as background to the various controversies in which he involved himself. It is the 1844 enquiry that is the raison d'être of this narrative, and the material on Duke's antiquarian activities and his time on the bench serve mainly to illustrate his quirky personality, although his extraordinary theory of Stonehenge is worthy of record on its own account. I did wonder whether I had devoted too much effort to an analysis of some of the absurdities in *Druidical Temples*, but took comfort in the words of the review of the book by William Maskell:

> Mr Duke has adventured too great an experiment upon the [supposed] ignorance and credulity of modern readers to pass his book over—as we had intended—with a single sentence of condemnation.

So if it is not a biography, and it is clear from the record that Mr Duke was neither a great achiever nor a great villain, and had few attributes in which anyone might be interested other than being a consummate troublemaker, why have I gone to all the effort of doing the research and writing it up? The original motivation was to finish the work started by my father. It was to be an *homage*, a memorial to him and the time and effort he expended in his investigations, and his many years as a regular at the British Museum Reading Room where he did his writing. But as my own researches progressed and details of the quite extraordinary behaviour of Mr Duke began to emerge, the narrative took on a momentum of its own. Duke's bizarre theory of Stonehenge and other Wiltshire monuments was not so remarkable for the time, coming as it did from a country clergyman with time on his hands. Oddities in his behaviour at the Quarter Sessions could be put down to a certain eccentricity of character. But his eight-year campaign against the Amesbury Union, and latterly the Poor Law Commissioners, was surely unique for its relentlessness, ferocity, and lack of cohesion. Whether or not it was true that he had never been heard to say a bad word to any member of his household, he would accuse individuals of wrong-doing based on the flimsiest of evidence, and was impervious to the concept of decision-making by majority vote. That people like Duke were, nevertheless, able to hold important positions, unchallenged for decades, and influence the daily lives and livelihoods of hundreds of people, needs to be placed on record.

Mr Duke certainly stress-tested the Poor Law Commission and, in an indirect way, might even have contributed to its downfall; this may be of interest to students of the Poor Laws. What is clear from Duke's campaign against the Amesbury Union, is that the Poor Law Commissioners were quite incapable of dealing with what was effectively a rogue guardian. In this respect the Poor Law Amendment Act itself was probably at fault in the restrictions it placed on the commissioners, as well as the apparent invulnerability enjoyed by the ex officio guardians.

A final reason that I think justifies the effort expended in the current work, is what it reveals about the workhouse in general, and the Amesbury Union Workhouse in particular. The Victorian workhouse has had a very bad press. It was the universal 'bogeyman' of the nineteenth century—even the early twentieth century; entering the workhouse was seen as a humiliating disgrace, only slightly less degrading than prison. The intention of the architects of the scheme was that the workhouse should be seen as a place of last resort, with strict rules and minimal food and clothing provided. A letter to *The Times* in 1836, no doubt from an unsympathetic ratepayer, stated that the workhouse should be 'held "in terrorem" over the idle and dissipated'.* There were stories of misery and deprivation, cruelty and abuse in workhouses, and many people would sooner die in the streets or fields than enter into one. The newspapers, those that disapproved of the New Poor Law, regularly printed stories of the destitute dying in misery because they had been refused assistance outside of the workhouse. But at the risk of giving away the ending of this story, if the evidence of many of the inmates is to be believed, the Amesbury Workhouse at least appeared to be a safe and sympathetic refuge for the poor. It is appropriate, therefore, to place on record first-hand evidence that there was there a place of real sanctuary for the young, old, destitute, and infirm. The inmates at all workhouses were clothed, fed, housed, and given access to healthcare, and the children were educated in 'reading, writing, arithmetic, and the principles of

---

* The paupers' 'work' in a workhouse varied according to its geographical location. The women generally did domestic chores like cleaning, cooking, and laundering, and sometimes also spinning and weaving and other craft activities. The men could be used for agricultural work, or other low-skill manual tasks like stone-breaking and oakum-picking. From workhouse. org.uk

the Christian religion'. The sexes were segregated, intoxicating liquors were strictly forbidden as were cards and dice, but the general workhouse rules did not forbid tobacco, although smoking inside the house was not allowed and matches were forbidden to the inmates.* It is abundantly clear from the testimony of many witnesses that there was also cleanliness and order, even an element of comfort, at Amesbury, and it was superintended by a sympathetic master and mistress. If proof were needed that the education was effective, there was ample evidence from the younger witnesses during the 1844 enquiry. Most of the paupers signed their testimony with an 'X', but the majority of the young inmates were able to sign their names, and in handwriting far superior to that of Assistant Poor Law Commissioner Parker.

---

\* The rules also allowed, at the discretion of the guardians, for infirm or aged married couples to have separate private rooms.

## Antiquarian Man of Letters

I f Edward Duke had never existed, it seems unlikely that even that master of bizarre characterization, Charles Dickens, would have been able to have invented him. When Duke could not get his way during meetings of the Amesbury Union guardians, which was most of the time, he would write to the Poor Law Commissioners. When their responses failed to satisfy him, he wrote personally to the chairman of the commissioners. And when the chairman had had enough of him, he wrote directly to the Home Secretary. Edward Duke elevated telling tales out of school into an art form.

However, if Mr Duke was not good at making friends and influencing people, he was very fortunate in his family circumstances. As the second son, of the fourth son, of a second son, his chances of the family manors of Lake, and Salterton and Newtown—together with the substantial Elizabethan mansion of Lake House—coming his way should have been small. But just like the D'Ascoynes in *Kind Hearts and Coronets*, one after another those ahead of him expired—although there was no suggestion that he accelerated the process. When his father's cousin, Robert Duke, who had inherited the manors and house, died without issue, Edward's father, Edward Duke senior, became the next in line, his three elder brothers having predeceased him. Robert Duke's marriage settlement allowed his wife Jane to enjoy the income from the land during her lifetime, so Edward Duke senior was never able to benefit from the inheritance and died in 1797. Since Edward junior's elder brother George had died even before their father, the young

Edward, aged twenty-six, inherited the manors and Lake House following Jane's death in 1805.

Edward Duke was born in Hungerford in 1779, the second son of Edward Duke and Fanny, née Field. They lived in a large house at twenty-six High Street, Hungerford, where Edward Duke senior practised as a surgeon. His wife Fanny was an heiress to property in Islington and in and around Hungerford, and it is likely that they had her to thank for the substantial family home. Edward Duke was their fifth child and second son. He grew up with elder brother George and five sisters. In 1794 when George died, Edward became his father's heir. Three years later Edward Duke senior died, and his son found himself at the age of eighteen not only owner of the house at Hungerford, but heir to the Duke family estates. Two years after that, he went up to Oxford to be provided with the education appropriate to his new status.

Edward Duke graduated BA at Magdalen Hall in 1803, and MA in 1807. Before graduating he received Holy Orders, and was subsequently a curate at Turkdean in Gloucester and then at Salisbury. However, following the inheritance of Lake House and the manors, Duke appears to have largely given up the active cure of souls. He performed the occasional marriage ceremony, and from time to time preached sermons in Salisbury. In 1806, now firmly ensconced in Lake House, which was about two miles from Stonehenge, he became actively interested in the prehistory and archaeology of Wiltshire. About a mile and a half north west of Lake House on Lake Downs, which Duke owned, stood a group of tumuli known as the 'Prophet Barrows', so called because in 1710 a group of French religious fanatics preached from one of them. Mr Duke decided that he wanted to open the barrows and look for artefacts. William Cunnington and Sir Richard Colt Hoare were the experts in the field and had already opened quite a number of barrows in Wiltshire. Colt Hoare was a very wealthy baronet who owned the house and estate at Stourhead; in 1803 he was taken to see a tessellated Roman pavement that Cunnington had excavated, and was so impressed with his work that he agreed to pay the expenses of labourers for Cunnington's archaeology. Cunnington, a mercer by trade and self-taught archaeologist, supervised the actual digging. In March 1806, Duke wrote to Colt Hoare telling him that he planned to open the barrows on his land. In a letter to Cunnington, Colt Hoare wondered whether Duke and his men would have the patience required and might ask for assistance. In September Colt Hoare wrote again to Cunnington:

> Mr Duke is impatient to know when we begin our operations that he may take his first lesson. I think we must let him have one of our experienced men to show his apprentices the right path, as well as to prevent the interments, etc. being deranged and destroyed.

And in October:

> Mr Duke ... shall be happy to meet you on the morning of the 23rd ... he seems very anxious to obey orders, and I hope he will turn out an apt and useful coadjutor.

Colt Hoare was unable to join them due to bad health, but he reminded Cunnington that as Duke would have ownership of the finds he must bear the expenses of the dig, with the exception of the costs of Cunnington himself for which Colt Hoare would be responsible.

Cunnington took two of his men and met Mr Duke, spending several days with him opening a number of barrows. He then wrote back to Colt Hoare in sardonic vein:

> I have just returned from Lake Downs, and although I have been among the prophets, I have not caught the spirit of prophesy. (Stephen and John pretend to this gift, and predict that our new disciple will soon be tired of opening barrows)[*]. Voltaire says of the French prophets that they attempted to raise the dead; but Mr Duke and myself have actually done

---

[*] Stephen and John were Cunnington's assistants.

> what they attempted in vain; but I confess our raising the dead
> has led to no important discoveries.

There was someone else present at the opening of Mr Duke's barrows. Richard Fenton, a barrister, was a travelling companion of Colt Hoare. In his book, *A Tour in Quest of Genealogy*, he eulogised Cunnington in three sonnets on the occasion of the opening of the Prophet Barrows. The third one was entitled: 'On attending the Rev. Mr. Duke, to whom the above group of barrows belonged, to direct the three operations of opening them':

> Auspicious morn by prophets long foretold,
> To Sarum's plain once more that calls my friend,
> The dark sepulchral mysteries to unfold,
> And DUKE'S initiation to attend:

Evidently Mr Duke was a good pupil. After Cunnington had left him, he supervised the opening of twenty more barrows in short order and made some most interesting finds. Colt Hoare visited Lake House less than three weeks later to see them. He wrote to Cunnington: 'We have just seen Mr Duke's museum, which is the most valuable I believe, that was ever collected in so short a space of time'. The finds consisted of pottery, jewellery, and four small rectangular 'counters', three with enigmatic designs, which Colt Hoare described as 'the conjuror's plaything'; they were possibly used for divination. He noted Mr Duke's archaeological findings in his *Ancient History of South Wiltshire*, first published in 1812, including a full-page illustration.

Edward Duke claimed friendship with Colt Hoare, who was a most notable antiquary, author, and landowner, and it seems likely that he wished to emulate him and cultivate his society. Whether they were really friends given Duke's quirky personality is a moot point. They were certainly acquainted and served on at least one committee together, but a remark in one of Colt Hoare's letters to Cunnington suggests that 'friendship' was perhaps stretching the reality of their relationship. Colt Hoare wrote: 'You have had a lucky Ducal escape—and you have been right in refusing the account of Stonehenge'. What event this enigmatic remark refers to is not known, but the date, September 1807, is sufficiently close to the opening of the Prophet Barrows to suggest that 'Ducal' quite probably referred to Edward Duke.

Stimulated by his success as an antiquarian and archaeologist, Duke was elected a fellow of the Society of Antiquaries in 1807, and of the Linnean Society in 1810; he was also a member of the Archaeological Institute of Great Britain and Ireland. In 1811, he opened seven further barrows near Durnford, although they contained just cremation urns. Colt Hoare in his book, commenting on Mr Duke's archaeological endeavours, observed:

> I am happy to think that the zeal he shewed in his first antiquarian researches was so amply remunerated, as to induce him to resume them on some future occasion.

It is possible to detect a mildly patronising tone here, suggesting that Duke was not quite 'one of us'. And just as Stephen and John had predicted, Mr Duke now seemed to tire of practical archaeology, although he may just have run out of barrows to excavate. In any event, a new project was beckoning. In January 1813, Edward Duke, 'a single man in possession of a good fortune', married Harriet Hinxman.* The groom was thirty-four, the bride, twenty-five. The ceremony was conducted at Alderbury, Harriet's place of birth, by her father, Henry Hinxman; he was curate of Nunney in the county of Somerset, and subsequently an alderman of Salisbury and a Wiltshire magistrate.

Edward Duke embraced his new project with enthusiasm, Harriet producing eight children over the next eleven years.

---

\* Just about this time, the first edition of *Pride and Prejudice* was going to the printers.

Harriet Hinxman was a good choice for a wife, because not only did she provide Mr Duke with the children he needed to carry on the line, but her father was a wealthy man. When he died in 1829 he left upwards of £17,000, equivalent to £1,700,000 in modern money, around a third of which came in the direction of the Rev Edward Duke's wife and children.

Edward Duke was now a well-established family man, and was able to turn his attention to other matters. *The Bath Chronicle* of 8 August 1816, reported that the Rev Edward Duke of Lake had qualified to act as a magistrate for Wiltshire at the Warminster Quarter Sessions. As well as his normal duties as a magistrate, Mr Duke was a fairly regular attendee at the Quarter Sessions, following them as they rotated between Salisbury, Warminster, Devizes, and Marlborough. He also found time to indulge his literary ambitions.

There is no record of what Mr Duke studied at Oxford but, judging from the period when he was there and the content of his subsequent writings, it was undoubtedly the Classics. He was steeped in the writings of the Greek and Roman historians, philosophers, and poets, and would frequently quote a whole sentence in Latin without translation.

In view of his later correspondence on antiquarian matters, it is curious that Duke appeared not to have written up his findings from opening the tumuli on Lake Downs. These were his own original work and significant enough to be included by Colt Hoare in his history of the county. It may be that at the time, and with his Oxford MA barely under his belt, Mr Duke lacked the confidence to do so.

His first foray into print appears to have been a letter written to the *Gentleman's Magazine* in 1814. This erudite journal, target audience 'educated and male', had been started in 1722 and, for a period in the 1740s, Dr Johnson was a frequent contributor. The founder and original editor was Edward Cave who used the nom de plume 'Sylvanus Urban'; letters were always addressed to *Mr Urban*, which name appears to have been adopted by subsequent editors. Mr Duke was responding to a request in a letter to confirm the text of the inscription on the tombstone in Hungerford of a Mr Greatrakes, who had apparently died in that town on his way from Bristol to London. Duke had grown up in Hungerford, so he was well qualified to respond. It must have been with mixed feelings that he saw his letter printed immediately after a note from Colt Hoare who was responding to the same request. To be seen in print alongside his hero must have been a thrill, mitigated by the fact that Colt Hoare had diluted his thunder. In a sense though, Duke did have the last laugh; never a person to use one word where ten would suffice, his letter occupied a good page and a half of the magazine, whereas Colt Hoare's was barely half a page long. Mr Duke's next contribution, in 1823, followed after a gap of nearly ten years and was on the subject of Stonehenge. Since that correspondence led eventually to his second book, *The Druidical Temples of the County of Wilts*, which was not published until 1846, it is appropriate to consider them together and describe initially his first book.

Commencing in December 1836, a large number of advertisements started to appear mainly in the Wiltshire newspapers for a book, newly published, entitled: *Prolusiones Historicae, or Essays Illustrative of The Halle of John Halle*, Vol I. The author was the Rev Edward Duke, MA, FAS & LS, and the title translates: 'Preliminary Historical Essays Illustrative of the Hall of John Hall'. John Hall, or Halle, had been a Salisbury wool merchant in the fifteenth century whose 'Hall' still existed in the city, and Mr Duke had decided to research his life. Volume I consisted of six essays: On the Origin of Names, the Family of John Halle, Origin of Heraldry and Halle's arms, Origin of Merchant's Marks, Fashion and Halle's Dress, and Memorials of Halle. A measure of the detail included can be ascertained from the fact that just a description of the contents of essay number five on dress, took seven pages.

A copy of the book in the Wiltshire and Swindon History Centre contains some notes on Mr Duke written in the flyleaf by a previous owner, T B Heathcote, dated 5 March 1903. He stated that the author lost money on the publication and never published volume II. He also transcribed a letter from Mr Duke, evidently to the first owner of the book, Mr T G B Estcourt, to whom it was a present. Estcourt had just resigned as chairman of the Wiltshire magistrates after thirty years, to be replaced by the person who was Mr Duke's arch-enemy, Mr Ludlow Bruges, and Estcourt was not one of Mr Duke's supporters on the bench.* The letter is quite illuminating:

T G B Estcourt Esq., Estcourt House
Lake House Nr Amesbury, Dec 31st 1836

My Dear Sir,

From the interest you have always taken in the Halle of John Halle, from my last conversation in the magistracy with you and from the personal regard I have for you, I beg your acceptance of the accompanying copy of my book.

It is strictly an antiquarian work, but I have made it my great object to produce an amusing book. I would recommend you first to read (which many people omit to do) the preface as that lets you into the scope of the work.

You will find the memorial of John Halle very interesting, but as the author I candidly say that I consider the gem of my book to be the dissertation on the pictures of St Christopher.

When you have read as much of the book as suits your fancy I hope to have your frank opinion of it, and if you should perchance to approve it (I give you a very emphatic if), I hope your patronage among your friends, as I have got some long bills staring me in the face which I want to knock heels over head. I am very nervous also for my credit.

---

* Mr Duke's difficulties with Mr Estcourt and Mr Ludlow Bruges are elucidated in the chapter on Duke's activities on the bench.

Under the present situation I did have a transient doubt whether I was right to make this little gift, lest it might be supposed I wished to neutralize you as an opponent, but on consideration I determined not to deprive myself of this pleasure, as I well knew that we are both too independent not to pursue our own ways.

I am Dear Sir, yours very truly, Edward Duke[*]

That Duke lost money on the book is not surprising, although it is difficult to believe that it placed him in any significant financial difficulty, because in a very real sense *Prolusiones Historicae* verges on the unreadable. The style is tediously affected and self-congratulatory, and the essays wander off on tangents, such that it is quite easy to forget the subject at hand. Furthermore, some of the writing is risible to a degree of absurdity. From pages 107—108:

> In my elucidation of the **Dress** of **John Halle**, where, gentle reader, shall I begin?—at the head?—or—at the feet?—but, since the head is the more noble part of man, and, as in travelling, the *descent* is ever the more easy, I will e'en at once proceed to the discussion of

**The Hat, Feather, and Brooch**[†]

He then proceeded to devote ten pages to a description of hats, five pages to feathers, eleven pages to brooches, and for good measure, thirty-seven pages to hair and beards.

The *Devizes and Wiltshire Gazette* of 4 January 1838 ran an advertisement placed by Mr Duke in which he listed extracts from a number of reviews of his book; a later insertion extended this number to fourteen. By looking at such of the originals

---

[*] The original letter may have been tucked into the book and Heathcote transcribed it because Mr Duke's handwriting was somewhat difficult to read.

[†] In Duke's book, the words in bold type reproduced here were printed in bold, gothic type which cannot but have considerably increased the cost of production; it also had at least two full colour illustrations.

that can be found and noting comments not reproduced, it is possible to form a more or less balanced and contemporary view of his work. There were some criticisms, although a few of the reviews were very complimentary. Naturally Mr Duke would not use any that were openly hostile, but a search has failed to discover any that were so.

The reviews of *Prolusiones Historicae* vary in length from a few lines in John Bull to sixteen pages in *The Monthly Review*, the latter of which must have gladdened Mr Duke's heart. Its praise was gushing:

> As a literary performance, few of our modern historical romances are half so much worth being read. Certainly we have never encountered any antiquarian disquisitions that were so amusing, delightful, and instructive ... there is nothing pompous, obscure or useless in the present work.

*John Bull* was terse and somewhat ambiguous:

> This work deserves a place among the curiosities of literature ... although we cannot but doubt whether the subject is altogether worth the pains and trouble which have been bestowed on it.

Several of the reviews expressed a similar sentiment. *The Spectator* devoted the best part of a page to a review, declaring the book to be 'quite a curiosity of literature'. Sections of the book were described, although at one point the reviewer observed:

> All this, it may be said, is a trivial base of facts on which to found a superstructure of 600 pages: but John Hall is only a peg on which to hang a great deal of antiquarian gossip.

That Mr Duke lost money on the book can be reliably ascertained from the fact that in spite of some apparently 'good' reviews, volume II was never published.

For a few years, Mr Duke's pen was exclusively occupied in writing letters, mostly to the Poor Law Commissioners. But in 1840, his grand theory of Stonehenge had its first outing. This work quite definitely owed its genesis to his extensive correspondence with the *Gentleman's Magazine* which had started seventeen years earlier.

Although Duke's first letter had appeared in 1814, it was between 1823 and 1829 that the bulk of his correspondence was published. In 1823, a certain 'A.H.' had written to the journal with some observations on Stonehenge. The correspondence which followed carried on in various forms for several years, and in it can be detected some of Mr Duke's later ideas concerning Stonehenge, Avebury, and Silbury Hill.

The origins of Stonehenge and other ancient monuments and their relationship to the Druids were intimately dissected and, since this relationship was taken by many as fact, it is appropriate to mention briefly what evidence existed for it. Virtually all that is known of the Druids in ancient times, i.e. at or before the time of the Romans in Britain, comes from the writings of that period—mainly Julius Caesar, Tacitus, and Pliny the Elder. Barry Cunliffe writes:

> The Druids were philosophers, teachers, judges, the repository of communal wisdoms about the natural world and the traditions of the people, and the mediators between humans and the gods.

Caesar claimed that Druidism originated in Britain, but the Druids left no written records and virtually no archaeological evidence. Since none of the ancient writers mentioned Stonehenge, there was nothing at all to connect it to the Druids.

It was the antiquarian John Aubrey, writing in the seventeenth century, who first suggested that Stonehenge and Avebury predated the Romans. Since the Druids were known to have been in Britain before the Romans, as the classical writers had claimed, it was not a great leap of imagination to assume that the stone circles were their temples. Other antiquaries  built on this, but it was William Stukeley in the eighteenth century, who with his writings created a positive

Druidic industry. After Stukeley, no-one could doubt that the Druids had built Stonehenge and the stone circles at Avebury and elsewhere, and used them for their rituals. It is interesting to note that Colt Hoare in his book on the history of Wiltshire declined to accept this theory. He wrote (in respect of Stonehenge etc.):

> The general title of Druidical has been given to all these stone monuments: and some of my readers may be surprized that I have not adopted it.

He quoted the 'learned' Mr Bryant: 'Under the sanction of their names we shelter ourselves, whenever we are ignorant and bewildered.' He also quoted Borlase: 'that the work of Stonehenge must have been that of a great and powerful nation, not of a limited community of priests'.

Edward Duke responded to A.H.'s remarks on Stonehenge in the *Gentleman's Magazine*, pointing out that most of what he said was incorrect. He did concede that the ancient authors had described the Druids as worshipping in 'woods and groves', which were not in evidence around Stonehenge and similar stone circles, and was unable to offer an explanation.* Subsequently, A.H. thanked Mr Duke 'for his judicious and explanatory answers'.

Mr Duke did make two further interesting comments: at least twice he said that he refrained 'at present' from imparting his own ideas as to the origin and nature of Stonehenge, but he also referred to the theory of Henry Browne of Amesbury, currently 'in the press'. Browne was, or was to be, the first guardian of Stonehenge, and had produced some models of the monument both as it was assumed to have been, according

---

* The historian Pliny the Elder had written that the Druids regarded oak groves as sacred, as was the mistletoe growing on oak trees which they harvested using a golden sickle, a ritual faithfully followed by the Druid Panoramix in the *Asterix* books.

to Stukeley, and in its current ruined state.* Browne's theory was that Stonehenge predated The Flood. His thesis was that since the ground sloped down from the south-west towards the monument, and it showed most damage in that quarter with stones leaning in the opposite direction, this could have been caused by a vast torrent of water flowing down the hill. In one sense, his theory could be said to have been viable; in the seventeenth century, Archbishop Ussher in his demonstration that the world was created in 4004 BC, had dated The Flood to around 2,300 BC, somewhat after the great sarsen stones were erected at Stonehenge.

Anyone with common sense, some knowledge, and a little judgement and insight is entitled to put forward a theory of Stonehenge—and countless have, although 'common sense, knowledge, judgement, and insight' are frequently missing. Browne's ideas did show imagination, and at the time the overwhelming majority of persons would have regarded the *Old Testament* as the unquestioning truth with which any theory of prehistory would have to be consistent. Mr Duke, however, was not yet ready to show his hand, and proceeded to debate the options with his fellow correspondents in the *Gentleman's Magazine*.

Over the next six years, a number of others entered the fray, some signing their names, some using aliases, and some just initials. There were two main topics of contention. Firstly, much ink was expended on the etymological analysis of the names of the various stone circles, tumuli, ditches, and banks in an attempt to associate them with different Celtic and Roman gods, and thereby gain some insight as to their purpose. Secondly, there was an ongoing debate regarding the problem of reconciling the stone circles as temples of the Druids, with what the classical writers had stated about their worshipping in

---

* The models were fabricated from cork, and sold for three-and-a-half guineas each.

oak groves. Various theories were offered in explanation, none of them very convincing. Mr Duke participated enthusiastically in the debate.

After a five-page letter in the September 1824 edition of the magazine on the interpretation of an 'Alabaster sculpture representing the Personification of the Holy Trinity', Mr Duke returned to the question of Stonehenge and the Druids the following month. He began modestly:

> In my letter of the 11th of March last ... I flatter myself, that the many arguments I advanced tended to demonstrate that ... Stonehenge (generally considered Druidical) was not, *in origine sua* [originally], surrounded by woods and groves.

He summarized the arguments, adding that if the Romans had cut down the sacred groves around the stone circles in an attempt to destroy the Druidic place of worship (one of the offered explanations), why did they not pull down the stone circles themselves? His letter was continued in the November edition. And now Mr Duke broke ranks with the received wisdom; apparently coming to the obvious solution to the conundrum (and agreeing with Colt Hoare) he wrote:

> I thus beg leave to express my doubts, my strong doubts, whether any of these stone temples *are* Druidical. This general opinion of course includes Stonehenge.

Mr Duke's next major foray on the subject of 'The supposed Druidical Monuments in Wiltshire' was addressed to the *Gentleman's Magazine* in June 1827. He was responding to a review of a pamphlet published by Reverend William Bowles in which the etymology of the names of various Wiltshire monuments was discussed. William Bowles had been educated at Winchester and Oxford, and was Vicar of Bremhill, not far from Avebury and Silbury Hill. He is, or was, mainly known as a poet, having published an edition of Alexander Pope, but an interest in the environs of his parish led him into antiquarianism. In 1828 he published *The Parochial History of Bremhill*, which included speculations on the origins of Avebury, Silbury Hill and the Wansdyke.

One exchange serves to illustrate what became a dispute, and also demonstrates Mr Duke's ability to latch on to a hypothesis entirely lacking in either plausibility or common sense and defend it to the last. Bowles had said in his book that the Wansdyke was a defensive barrier running east-west, 'the last frontier ramparts of the encampments of the Belgae northwards', dating from not long after the departure of the Romans; this was the received wisdom. Mr Duke, after advancing some rather questionable arguments against this hypothesis and much etymological analysis, suggested that it was one of the 'four great highways' of Edward The Confessor. Bowles responded:

> No argument can induce me to think it was ever intended for a road, for these reasons: 1st It comes from no distinguished station or city and leads to none ... 2nd In many parts, two wheel-barrows could not pass!! 3rd It has a vallum [a defensive wall] very like a rampart; in some places nearly forty feet high.

Over the next two years, Bowles and Duke sparred in the pages of the *Gentleman's Magazine* until the editor called a halt to the correspondence. In the edition for February 1829, he declined to publish the latest letter from Mr Duke, suggesting that he and Bowles settle the matter in the latter's dining room. No doubt Duke was furious and thought that he had been snubbed, and it was twenty years before anything of his appeared in the journal again.

Given the intensity, and density, of material related to Stonehenge etc. that had formed Duke's *Gentleman's Magazine* correspondence, it is odd that he delayed writing up his theory for more than ten years, doing the research and writing for *Prolusiones Historicae* first. It is possible that he was so upset at his last letter not being published, that he set it all aside in a huff. What started him off again much later may simply have been a happy accident: the request from a friend and fellow author for assistance.

Between February and August 1840, Mr Duke's grand theory on the origin of Stonehenge, Avebury, and Silbury Hill was published in weekly instalments in the *Salisbury and Winchester Journal*. In an introductory note on 10 February, Mr Duke stated that a friend of his, the author of a book, *The Barrow Diggers*, 'lately published', had requested him to bring the book to the notice of the public. However, 'prior to any remarks specially on it, I have found it necessary to offer a preliminary dissertation of some length'. This preliminary dissertation occupied a column or so of the newspaper for the next twenty-five weeks. The editor dutifully headed each week's offering 'The Barrow Diggers', although after twenty-two weeks this was dropped to be replaced with 'Stonehenge', when it became clear that Mr Duke had entirely lost sight of the original reason for his dissertation. After the first week, he made no more mention of his friend's book. The readers of the newspaper were given no further information about *The Barrow Diggers*, than that it was published by Shipp of Blandford, and was the work of a gentleman who had 'modestly withheld his name from the world'.

Quite what the gentleman, whose name was Charles Woolls, thought of this curious behaviour on the part of his supposed friend has not been recorded. Charles Woolls was a graduate of Pembroke College, Oxford, ordained deacon in 1826, and priest in 1828. In 1826 he was appointed curate to Sturminster Marshall, and in 1834 rector to Charborough. On the title page, *The Barrow Diggers* is described as 'A Dialogue in imitation of the grave-diggers in Hamlet', which had been written after the author 'had assisted an exceedingly agreeable party' in opening a barrow.* The 'agreeable party' may have

---

* The 'Barrow Diggers' were the people excavating the barrows, not the ancients who originally constructed them.

been Thomas Rackett who was a notable antiquary and the rector of Spetisbury, adjacent to Sturminster Marshall, to whom the volume was dedicated. The dialogue occupies the first third of the book, while the rest of the work consists of a series of notes with illustrations and a review of the nature of barrows and their contents. Mr Duke, 'the amusing and ingenious author of *Prolusiones Historicae*', was mentioned several times, as were Colt Hoare, William Cunnington, and several others involved in excavating barrows.

*The Barrow Diggers* received several very positive reviews in the local newspapers when it was published, including one in the *Salisbury and Winchester Journal*. Perhaps Mr Duke was contacted as a person with experience opening barrows although that had been nearly thirty years previously; Colt Hoare and Cunnington, who were very experienced barrow diggers, were both dead by this time. Charles Woolls was keen to get some publicity for his book and hoped that Duke would oblige. But Mr Duke was apparently interested only in his own ideas. He forged ahead with the exposition of his grand theory, commenting at one point on the difficulty of producing copy to meet the weekly schedule required by the newspaper.

After a few paragraphs on the different countries where barrows or 'sepulchral tumuli' are to be found, Mr Duke noted that they are 'nowhere in greater numbers than in Wilts ... Hants and Dorset'. He also noted their presence in numbers 'around the temples of Abury* and Stonehenge', adding that 'mention of Stonehenge leads me at present necessarily to digress from the immediate subject of tumuli or barrows'. It was to be a lengthy digression, barrows hardly getting any further mention, because Mr Duke became entirely focused on his theory of Stonehenge.

Before describing Duke's 1840 theory in detail, it is appropriate to consult the second outing of his ideas. This

---

\* In Mr Duke's time, Avebury was generally known as 'Abury'.

resulted from the gathering together of many of the weekly episodes from the *Salisbury and Winchester Journal*. A book version, *The Druidical Temples of the County of Wilts, was* published six years later; it included much material taken verbatim from the newspaper. What is odd though, is that in his 1840 theory Mr Duke declared, with 'proofs', what he had already said in two of his letters to the *Gentleman's Magazine*, that the Druids did not construct Stonehenge—contradicting Stukeley and many others, but agreeing with Colt Hoare. In the 1846 version, he says with just as much vigour that they did construct it. Furthermore, he made no mention of his earlier contrary assertion, or even that he had changed his mind. Here is Mr Duke in the 1840 newspaper version:

> I doubt much whether Druidism was ever the general religion of Britain or of Gaul. I doubt much whether the Druids ever existed on the Salisbury Plain, or worshipped at Stonehenge. The testimony even of Caesar and Pliny, as to these Priests, may well be doubted.

He rejected Caesar's account of the Druids since he had had to use an interpreter to talk to them; Pliny he also rejected because of his 'so many wonderful stories'. He did not believe the accounts of human sacrifice by fire (the notorious 'Wicker Man'), and he did not believe the accounts of the Druids cutting mistletoe with golden sickles. He declared that 'Misseltoe ... grows abundantly on the apple and thorn; but is not found on the oak', and added, 'nor will gold, the most ductile and pliant of all metals, be made, in its native state, to assume the power of cutting', which was quite true. He appeared to accept the account of Caesar, that the Druids worshipped in 'woods and groves', as proof that they did not build Stonehenge. It and the other ancient monuments were always found in open country. He 'boldly proclaim[ed]':

> in my opinion, with the Druids, and with the Belgae (the *supposed* Roman inhabitants of Wilts), the Segontiaci, the

Bibroci, the Attrebates &c. &c. these venerable and remote temples had nought to do.

The actual builders of Stonehenge etc. were, he said, colonists 'roaming from the east' from countries bordering Egypt and Phoenicia, bringing a knowledge of 'astronomy ... arithmetic ... and mechanics' to the British Isles, since 'Egypt was ever considered as the cradle of arts and sciences'. It was the Phoenicians much later, he said, who introduced Druidism into the western part of the British Isles. In summary then, in Duke's 1840 theory published in the newspaper, the Druids had nothing to do with Stonehenge, they arrived long after it was built, and they certainly never worshipped there.

In his 1846 book Mr Duke offered quite a different version of events—the very title gives it away: *The Druidical Temples of the County of Wilts*. In chapter three, having said that Stukeley attributed Stonehenge and Avebury to the Druids, Duke declared: 'When I say, that Abury and Stonehenge were constructed by the Druids, I mean that they provided the master mind to plan and to direct'. He now believed that the Druids were the priests of the Sabaeans*, who worshipped the planets, and were brought to Britain by the Phoenicians. Regarding the ancient stone temples: 'to suppose temples without ... a priesthood, would be an absurdity ... and what should their priests be but Druids?' And now he seemed to have reversed his view of which parts of the ancient writers' works to believe:

> [the] ancient authors, who attribute to them manners and customs, to which, I am convinced, they were utter strangers; amongst other things they make them resort to woods and groves, and yet we find their temples in the most open and champain countries.

The identity of the builders of Stonehenge and the other monuments was central to Mr Duke's thesis, since knowing

---

* This had been suggested by a correspondent to the *Gentleman's Magazine.*

who they were, and their knowledge and beliefs, might illuminate the purpose of Stonehenge. It is certainly curious that he should not refer to his substantial change of mind in the 1846 book. It is also fairly clear that he had culled many of these ideas from the earlier correspondents' letters to the *Gentleman's Magazine*, where the origins of Stonehenge were extensively discussed.

Nevertheless, the nub of Duke's thesis was this: the Phoenicians—or someone else—had brought 'Chaldean' (Babylonian), or possibly Egyptian, astronomical knowledge to Britain, and the ancient Britons, be they Druids or no, using this knowledge had designed Avebury, Silbury Hill, Stonehenge, a minor stone circle at Winterbourne Bassett, and some earthworks in between, as a great stationary planetarium or orrery. Avebury was the temple of the Sun and the Moon, the twin smaller stone circles within the great circle representing those heavenly bodies, and the avenues represented the passage of the Sun and Moon through the ecliptic around Silbury Hill, which was the Earth. Other monuments represented the planets on a 16-mile meridian, with Stonehenge, the most southerly point, designated Saturn.[*] As justification for this theory, Mr Duke declared:

> these planetary temples were all located at due distances from each other ... the relative proportions of those distances correspond with those of the present received system; and ... in three instances, the sites of these temples bear in their names at this day plain and indubitable record of their primitive dedication.

Mr Duke's planetarium was the correct order of planets, but with the Earth at the centre, which was hardly the 'present

---

[*] One indisputable fact about Stonehenge, is that the main axis is aligned to the midsummer sunrise and midwinter sunset. If it is anything, Stonehenge should be a temple of the Sun. Mr Duke acknowledged that it was also a temple of the Sun, but failed to explain how it could be associated with both the Sun and Saturn.

received system' where the planets revolve around the sun. He did not give the relative proportions of the actual solar system for comparison, and failed to mention the difficulty of reconciling planetary distances where the Sun is at the centre, with those where the Earth was at the centre. The 'indubitable record' of ancient names appeared to consist of three items: a translation of *Abiri* (Abury) in Hebrew and Arabic as 'Mighty Ones'; an earthwork at the village of Marden = *'Mars Den'* which he assigned to the planet Mars; and Knap Hill, adjacent to Walkers hill (the 'Temple of Mercury'), where Knap = Kneph, 'the Egyptian name for Mercury'. The most extraordinary claim in Mr Duke's theory related to the planet Saturn. He noted with astonishment that, since the ratio of the diameters of the stone circle at Stonehenge to its surrounding ditch was the same as that of Saturn to its rings, the ancients must have had telescopes and been able to see that planet's rings.

A viable theory unifying, and to some extent explaining, Stonehenge, Avebury, and Silbury Hill, the three great ancient structures in Wiltshire, was one of the Holy Grails of British archaeology and should have been met with universal interest and comment.* Furthermore, inspection of Mr Duke's plan does show some correlation between the relative distances of several of the monuments and those of their designated planets. He claimed, correctly, that the monuments certainly predated the Roman era, since no Roman artefacts had been found in excavations of them or the surrounding barrows; this was a point that had been the central discussion topic among the 'Barrow Diggers'. And he suggested, also correctly, that the monuments were contemporaneous with the pyramids.

As justification for his findings, Mr Duke offered a wealth of classical and Biblical references, and etymological and numerical analysis, all of which would require a scholar of

---

* The fact that it wasn't, suggests that other antiquarians dismissed it out of hand.

those subjects to untangle. Considering just his astronomical alignments, there are major difficulties with the theory. The ancients had no idea of the relative *distances* of the planets; that was not established until the seventeenth century. Only their *order* from the Earth was known, and that had been worked out by the Greeks, and possibly the Babylonians before them, based on the planetary periods. The idea that Avebury with its twin circles represented the sun and the moon, which appear to be the same size from Earth, had been mooted by Stukeley 100 years earlier. But if the system really was *designed*, why was the brightest planet, Venus, represented by a rough stone circle at Winterbourne Bassett, when a minor and irregular shaped earthwork at Casterly Camp was used for the second brightest planet, Jupiter? And how could a long barrow on Walkers Hill represent Mercury? These three structures are each of an entirely different type.[*]

Many of Mr Duke's propositions and arguments are absurd. For example, he repeated an idea that Bowles had treated with amused disbelief in the *Gentleman's Magazine* correspondence. Duke had suggested that the ancient Britons had connected one village with another using a 'fosse', four or five feet deep and around three feet wide at the bottom, such that the chalk thrown up would 'light unto their paths' at night enabling them to travel between them. But it was his suggestion, and refutation, of a possible objection to the attribution of Silbury Hill as the Earth in his planetarium, that was a masterclass of plain confusion and foolishness. From Tomlinson's book on astronomy, see below, Duke had learned that the Earth has the shape of an oblate spheroid, which is a sphere squashed along its north-south axis, shaped like a pumpkin. The amount of 'squashing', the difference in the Earth's radius at the equator and the poles, is very small

---

[*] See Fig 5 for the relative size, shape and character of the elements of Mr Duke's planetarium.

and amounts to approximately one part in 300, or around thirteen miles. This makes our planet indistinguishable from a true sphere to all but an advanced civilization with precision mapping and mature Newtonian mechanics. Nevertheless, Duke said:

> It has been observed to me that the shape of Silbury Hill militates against the supposition, that it was intended to represent the Earth. It is thus said that the form of the Earth is that of an oblate spheroid, whilst this hill presents the form of a cone ... The objection when duly considered, carries very little weight with it.

He ignored the painfully obvious fact that, given the extraordinary nature of his central tenet, the last objection anyone was likely to make to his theory was that a prehistoric representation of the Earth was not a perfect oblate spheroid. But even if such an objection had been raised, Mr Duke might have made the quite reasonable point that if the ancient Britons were faced with the task of representing a sphere, whether oblate or not, using the materials at hand—chalk, turf, wood and possibly some stone—they might have concluded that a conical hill would be a decent compromise between the ideal and the practical. Instead, he said that the geometry of the 'planetarium' demanded that Silbury Hill could not be placed anywhere else other than where it was, and that was in a 'hollow surrounded on all sides by moderately rising ground' and it needed to be 'visible from certain distances and certain points'. A perfectly fair argument; but then he made it clear that he had no idea of the actual form of an oblate spheroid, calling it at one point an 'oblong spheroid', the shape of a rugby ball, which is a *prolate* spheroid. He had totally confused the two, declaring of Silbury Hill:

> they [the ancients] might have made its base extend over ten acres of ground, and only raised it half its height ... they might thus have raised a hill somewhat in the form of an oblate spheroid, but then they would have hid it in a hollow!

His reasoning seemed to be that a rugby-ball shaped 'Earth' placed on its side would occupy a greater area, ten acres, but be lower, and therefore less visible, than Silbury Hill as built, whose base area was five-and-a-half acres.

There are many other objections to Duke's book, far too numerous to consider here, but two can be mentioned. During his studies of Stonehenge, he had recruited the help of Rev Lewis Tomlinson, a schoolteacher from Salisbury, to help him measure some angles between the various stones. It seems likely that Duke derived his knowledge of astronomy from Tomlinson's book, *Recreations in Astronomy*. The book is straightforwardly written, and an accessible introduction to the subject. The section on theories of the solar system covers Ptolemy, Copernicus, Tycho Brahe, and Newton, but unaccountably omits Kepler.[*] Duke's book also omits Kepler, and both accounts mention Tycho Brahe's somewhat irrelevant theory of the solar system. But then Duke made the extraordinary statement:

> In the fourteenth century arose up Copernicus[†], the author of the system now generally embraced, *but which, as I believe, is not yet established on the surest grounds* [Author's italics].

To suggest that Copernicus' heliocentric (sun-centred) theory of the solar system was 'not yet established on the surest grounds', given the state of knowledge of astronomy in the mid-nineteenth century, is absurd and betrays Duke's very tenuous grip on that subject. But the most obvious strain on credibility is his notion that Stonehenge represented Saturn, complete with its rings, which the ancients had been able to

---

[*]   It was Kepler who analysed twenty years' worth of Tycho Brahe's very accurate planetary sightings, and deduced that the orbits of the planets were ellipses rather than circles—a fact that Newton later proved mathematically. Kepler's laws allowed the relative distances of the planets from the sun to be computed for the first time.

[†]   Copernicus was actually born in the *fifteenth* century and his major work was published in the *sixteenth* century.

observe with telescopes. To support his theory, he quoted Strabo, first century AD, who had written: 'Vapours produce the same effect as the tubes in magnifying objects [of vision] by diffraction'. The implication is that Strabo was describing a telescope. In fact there is much evidence that lenses were known to the Greeks and even earlier civilizations. Lenses fabricated from rock crystal dating to 1,400 BC were said to have been discovered by Sir Arthur Evans at Knossos in Crete. The British Museum contains a similar type of lens found in the ruins of the palace at Nimrud on the Tigris dating to around 750 BC. Aristophanes, circa 420 BC, referred to a lens or burning glass in his play *The Clouds*, and Seneca the Younger, first century AD, described how small writing was enlarged when seen through a glass globe filled with water.

In Henry King's *The History of the Telescope*, it is stated that Hans Lippershey, who filed a patent for the telescope in 1607, came upon the basic principle from some children larking around with spectacle lenses in his shop. They had found that by placing one before the other they could magnify distant objects. Given that lenses did exist at the time of the Babylonians, it is not impossible that rudimentary telescopes could have been known at the time Stonehenge was built. But the military and seafaring benefits of telescopes would have been enormous, so it seems inconceivable that had they been known of and used, however momentous the secret, there would have been no unequivocal mention of the fact in the ancient texts, let alone the discovery of artefacts.

The well-documented history of telescope use also militates very strongly against Mr Duke's thesis. When Galileo, the pioneer of astronomical telescopic observation in the early seventeenth century, turned his telescope towards Saturn he was puzzled by what he saw; the planet appeared to have ears. He said: 'I have observed the highest of the planets three-formed.' He was even more puzzled when a few years later Saturn's rings had moved edge on and disappeared. It was not until several decades after that, in 1655, that the true nature of the rings was suggested by Huygens following observations with a much larger and more powerful telescope. Galileo's major discovery was that Jupiter had four moons; had the ancients possessed telescopes capable of seeing Saturn's rings, they would have been able to observe the far more obvious moons of Jupiter.* Not only would that have required considerable changes to their astronomy, but such a momentous discovery could hardly have failed to be manifest in the celebration of Jupiter in their religion and its representation in Mr Duke's so-called planetarium. Had he known a little more astronomy, he would have realized that.

There was no reaction to Mr Duke's 1840 theory in the newspaper other than a letter from a reader complaining that after twenty-six instalments, patiently read, there was no review of *The Barrow Diggers* which had been promised. Of *Druidical Temples*, which unlike *Prolusiones* received relatively little advertising in the press, there were a few descriptive reviews, but the *Christian Remembrancer* published an eleven-page excoriating and quite merciless analysis of the book by William Maskell. He wrote:

> It has seldom been our unhappy fate to wade through a book, in the pages of which we could find less instruction of any kind, or a larger number of the most puerile absurdities.

Maskell dismissed the book as 'twaddle', commenting: 'It is a curious fact that lunatics will never believe that they are insane'. He attacked Mr Duke for his lack of authorities and his absurd arguments, he mocked him for his style and for comparing himself favourably with Colt Hoare and Stukeley, and he ridiculed his lack of knowledge of astronomy. His theory of the Druids observing Saturn with a telescope was, he said, the book's 'crowning absurdity'. He pointed out

---

\* They would also have seen that Venus shows phases, just like the moon, in different parts of its orbit.

that Duke had talked about three instances of the names of his temples bearing 'plain and indubitable record of their primitive dedication', but he only ever detailed one in the book. In fact Duke *had* described all three, but only in the newspaper articles; he forgot, or failed to check, that this detail was not reproduced in the book. Maskell opined that Mr Duke was a young man who would realize the 'unreasonableness of his early speculations [after the] calmness of a matured manhood had sobered his youthful impatience'.*

Mr Duke was sixty-one years old when the newspaper instalments were printed and sixty-seven when his book was published, so 'youthful impatience' could not be used as an excuse. But he did possess a stubborn streak, bordering on the pathological, and was subject to petulance. This was clear from the press reports of his relationships with his fellow magistrates and Poor Law guardians. It may have been petulance that caused him to sever connections with his academic peers in 1829, when he took umbrage at the editor of the *Gentleman's Magazine* for not publishing his latest letter. If he had aired his theories in the pages of that journal, there is little doubt that the more absurd of his notions would have been condemned for what they were before they were committed to book form. Nevertheless, even several exchanges with Rev Bowles, who pointed out the preposterousness of Duke's theory on the Wansdyke, failed to stop him mentioning in his book the idea of a fosse as a roadway connecting villages—this Maskell had also mocked as demonstrating Mr Duke's 'qualification' to be 'the discoverer of the original purpose of Stonehenge'.

Edward Duke had one more foray into print; the December 1849 edition of the *Gentleman's Magazine* published his *Theory of Stonehenge* complete with two full-page pictures of the monument. It had taken twenty years to overcome his reluctance to communicate with the journal, although the effect

---

* It is possible that Maskell mistook Duke for his son, also Rev Edward Duke.

of Maskell's review of *Druidical Temples* was quite manifest. Duke's style was sober, modest, and restrained; he mentioned his book on Stonehenge only in passing, the purpose of the note being a numerological analysis of the stones and how this related to the divisions of a circle and various astronomical cycles. Even so, he continued to make foolish claims. He said: 'It is, I think, indisputable that the Druids divided the circumference of the globe into 360 degrees'.

The *Babylonians* certainly divided the circle into 360 degrees; Pliny had written that the Druids cut mistletoe on the 'sixth day of the moon', and 'by the moon … they measure their months and years and also their eras of thirty years', so they did possess some knowledge of astronomy. Whether they also divided the circle into 360 degrees is certainly not indisputable since they left no written records. Mr Duke had confused documented knowledge of the Babylonians, with his highly conjectured theories of the Druids. Even after the intellectual drubbing he had received from the *Christian Remembrancer*, he was still making foolish statements. There was no response in the journal to his piece.

# Justice of the Peace

**M**r Duke became a magistrate in 1816, and was to serve on the bench for twenty-eight years. For most of the time his performance was unremarkable enough, although he did have a knack for upsetting his fellow magistrates, and it was as a JP that he seems to have developed his talent for dispute and controversy. His name appeared regularly in the local newspapers reporting the various cases in which he was involved. Also reported were notable speeches at the Quarter Sessions, his attendance at dinners, his activities as visiting magistrate to the county gaol at Fisherton, and his presence at meetings of the 'Amesbury Association for the Prevention of Robberies and Thefts', of which he was vice president. In July 1834 a story was printed in the *Morning Chronicle*, describing an incident in which Mr Duke valiantly searched a house for an escaped prisoner.

The first whiff of controversy came in 1828 when Mr Duke denied George Atkinson, chief magistrate of Salisbury, further permission to visit two prisoners in the county gaol; he judged that Atkinson had disobeyed prison rules on religious instruction. Atkinson was deeply incensed and wrote an open letter, published in the *Salisbury and Winchester Journal*, detailing his grievances against Duke. A few years later, Mr Duke upset another magistrate, Mr Goodlake, in a row related to the repair, or rather the lack of it, to the road through some villages connecting Marlborough to Salisbury. Once more, an open letter printed in several newspapers was resorted to, and Mr Duke was criticised for resurrecting a matter that had already been decided twice by a large majority vote in two separate Quarter Sessions.

In 1835, a case at the Salisbury Assizes concerning a disputed will was reported in the London newspapers. Duke had been a witness for the defendant, who had won the case, and although his actions were not cited as grounds to overturn the verdict, they were extraordinary for a magistrate. He had been 'active in collecting evidence for the defendant' before the trial, and after the trial had ridden a horse in procession, decorated with 'ribands', declaring: 'We have gained the victory, we have gained the day'. And even though he was a witness, during the trial he had dined with some of the special jurymen.

Mr Duke seemed to have prevailed over Messrs Atkinson and Goodlake, and there was no record of a censure following his questionable behaviour at the Salisbury Assizes. But when he encountered Mr Ludlow Bruges over the question of the new assize courts, he more than met his match. William Heald Ludlow Bruges—'Bruges' was an adopted surname through the will of his great uncle—was Recorder of Devizes, and would be MP for Bath from 1837 to 1841, and Devizes from 1844 until 1848. The saga of Duke's implacable resistance to the moving of one of the assize courts illustrates rather well his character, as well as his standing among his peers in the Wiltshire magistracy.

In June 1835, an 'Order in [Privy] Council' required that henceforth the Wiltshire Assizes should alternate between Salisbury and Devizes; previously, both assize courts had always been held at Salisbury. The briefest glance at a map of Wiltshire shows that whereas Salisbury is at the south-eastern extremity of the county, Devizes is right in the centre. Locating at least one of the courts at Devizes would substantially decrease the travelling time for the majority of attendees, thereby increasing the convenience, and reducing the expense which the county had to bear. Naturally there were local interests involved. The presence of an assize court meant considerable business for local traders, innkeepers, and hoteliers. Ludlow Bruges was from Seend (four miles to the west of Devizes) and would be MP for Devizes eight years later. Edward Duke had a number of associations with the city of Salisbury; he lived barely eight miles from the city, had been a curate there, and still preached from time to time in the churches. Matters boiled over in the October Quarter Sessions held at Marlborough in 1836.

The proceedings were reported by the *Devizes and Wiltshire Gazette*, which noted the very large number of magistrates present. Mr Ludlow Bruges proposed the motion that the new court at Devizes should be conveyed to the county substantially free of charge, with just the outstanding cost of finishing the building, £807, to be debited to the county rates. He summarized the 1833 Act of Parliament that had prompted the building of the new court; he had organized a memorial signed by 3,000 people, including the majority of Wiltshire magistrates, requesting that the summer assizes be moved from Salisbury to Devizes. The order was duly made, the premises were built, financed by private subscription, and the summer court had already been held in Devizes in 1835 and 1836. Ludlow Bruges laid out the benefits. From the census returns, three quarters of the population of the county were closer to Devizes than Salisbury, and over the previous few years twice as many prisoners had been committed from places closer to Devizes. He estimated that prosecutors and witnesses had to travel an extra 10,000 miles for the Salisbury Assizes compared to Devizes, with the burden on the county of the extra travelling expenses and daily allowances that that entailed. The cost to the county of defraying the £807 he estimated to be equivalent to around one penny extra in every £6 5s of income from the rates. He commended the motion to the meeting, calling it a 'cheap, speedy, and effectual administration of justice'. After Mr Phipps seconded the motion, Mr Duke rose to speak against it. Duke and Ludlow

Bruges had already clashed on the subject during the January Quarter Sessions held at Devizes, when Duke had attempted to have the motion thrown out on a technicality. Ludlow Bruges had accused him of putting every obstacle in the way of the new court, including a 'private' communication to the 'Secretary of State'.[*]

Mr Duke claimed that he had always said that Devizes had a fair claim to the summer assizes, but doubted that the town had sufficient accommodation. He said he had frequently heard from the supporters of the motion that the county should not be put to one farthing expense for the new court (cries of "No! No!"), and he was surprised that they should now be seeking to put £800 on the county rate. He pointed out that the courts at Salisbury had recently been extended entirely at the expense of the 'inhabitants and gentlemen of the neighbourhood', and it was hard that they should now have to contribute to the new courts at Devizes. He then commented on the committee, chaired by Mr Ludlow Bruges, responsible for having the new court erected. He accused them of being a self-appointed junta, 'giving the Quarter Sessions the go-by'.[†] He would not, he said, submit to the affairs of the county being governed by a junta. Mr Ludlow Bruges had charged him with a secret communication with the Secretary of State—not so, since he had sent Ludlow Bruges a copy of the letter by the same post. He again accused the committee of being illegal, expressing surprise that someone as conversant with the rules as Ludlow Bruges should have countenanced it. He would vote against the motion.

Mr Methuen accused Mr Duke of an 'awful [and] mysterious' manner, and was sorry if the gentlemen from the south of the county could not see that those from the north

---

[*]    Presumably the Home Secretary.

[†]    A formal motion to establish the committee had failed since insufficient notice had been given; the majority wished it, so it went ahead in any case.

were seeking to 'save their pockets'. He pointed out that the holding of at least one assize at Devizes would save the amount in question. And it is interesting to note that no-one seemed to question the point, least of all Duke himself, that since the summer assizes had already been held twice in Devizes, the money ought to have been saved already; no increase in the rates ought, therefore, to have been necessary.

Several others spoke, mostly in favour of the motion, after which Mr Ludlow Bruges proceeded to dismantle Mr Duke and his objections piece by piece. The newspaper called it an 'able and masterly reply'. The new court was a great public benefit, he said, and the cost was 'adequate' to the benefit received. He claimed that much misrepresentation had taken place on the part of the opposition to the proposal, and in particular, many of Mr Duke's observations were erroneous. Mr Duke, he went on, said that he was written to for his opinion on the removal of the assizes; what he was actually written to for was a subscription, which he failed to provide, 'and he comes here today, and says that the whole expense should have been defrayed by subscription!' Cheering and much laughter greeted this last point. Bruges poured scorn on another of Duke's objections to the Devizes Court, namely that the building itself was unsafe because a building with a similar roof in his neighbourhood had collapsed; to much laughter and cheers, he pointed out that after nine months the building still stood 'as substantial as ever!' Finally, Ludlow Bruges said that Mr Duke had accused him and the committee of 'intrigue and impudent conduct'. He rejected the charge, saying that he and his colleagues had as much public virtue and spirit as Mr Duke and any of his colleagues, and disdained such conduct. He challenged Mr Duke whether he 'disdained such conduct', relating the contents of a letter Duke had addressed to him. In this letter, Mr Duke had apparently offered to support the bringing of all of the Quarter Sessions to Devizes, if Ludlow Bruges dropped the idea of bringing the summer assizes to that town! It was a fatal blow to Mr Duke; to have accused the other side of intrigue, and then to be shown to have been guilty of a far baser intrigue himself. The motion was put to the vote and carried by thirty-seven in favour with twelve against. Even the newspaper reporting the proceedings criticised Mr Duke. In the report, the *Devizes and Wiltshire Gazette* had inserted a comment to the effect that Mr Duke had behaved ungraciously towards them, accusing them in his speech of failing to report all that he had said the last time that he and Ludlow Bruges had clashed, when the newspaper had printed exactly what he had asked them to report.

At this point most people would have admitted defeat. The arguments in favour of the county taking ownership of the new assize court were unassailable. As far as Duke was concerned though, it was a point of principle, although many no doubt thought that it was just obstinate and vexatious bloody-mindedness. But Mr Duke was made of sterner stuff than to throw in the towel just because he had been shown to look foolish and devious in front of his peers. He retained the services of Sir William Follett, the Solicitor General in Robert Peel's government. Follett, MP for Exeter, and Attorney General in a later administration, was regarded as the finest advocate of his generation. Sir William was asked to rule whether the motion carried by a seventy-five per cent majority at the Marlborough Quarter Sessions was lawful, and on 8 December the *Devizes and Wiltshire Gazette* ran a brief editorial on his findings:

> We regret to find that the propriety of conveying the Assize Courts to the County is again to be agitated. The Rev. Mr. Duke, it will be seen, has taken Sir William Follett's opinion on the Order of last Session, and Sir William says the Order is bad. That the Rev. Mr. Duke is acting from a sense of duty, no one who knows him will dispute; but we apprehend that very few will give him credit for exercising sound judgement in this case.

Three weeks later the newspaper published a long open letter from Mr Duke on the subject, addressed to the 'Magistrates of North Wilts'. He summarized his opposition to the order and said that Sir William Follett had declared it to be invalid. He said that his character and honour had been assailed by his 'opponent', and that he had no power of reply. He claimed the 'rightful privilege of self-vindication,' demanding an 'impartial and attentive' hearing. However, he had received a letter suggesting that an attempt would be made to subvert this 'tribute of justice' by the 'clamours of party spirit'—Mr Duke was suggesting that he would be shouted down. If that were to be the case, he threatened that 'North Wilts will not wrest from me those documents which are my own private property'. Meaning, it is supposed, that he would not share Sir William Follett's findings, but rather take them to a higher court. He went on to insist that the outstanding amount needed to complete the new court, which he said was £1,200 not £807, should be raised by subscription from North Wiltshire, with no extra burden on the rates. Only then should the new courts be conveyed to the county. It is hard to understand why Mr Duke claimed that he had no power of reply, since he was as able to speak during the Quarter Sessions as anyone else, and had done so, as was attested by the newspaper reports. He was clearly of the opinion that the legal judgment of Sir William Follett was the magic bullet that would settle the matter once and for all.

In January 1837, a few days after the publication of Duke's open letter, the matter was discussed again at the Devizes Sessions. After strenuous opposition from Mr Duke, Ludlow Bruges was elected the new chairman of the sessions, the previous chairman, Mr T G B Estcourt, having resigned. Mr Methuen protested at Duke's language, and referring to his open letter said to loud cheers: 'Mr Duke had expressed his fears that he might be put down by clamour; and yet what a pretty example had he himself set!'

The question of the new assize court was now again discussed. Duke had the floor but, according to the press reports, 'appeared at a loss what course to pursue'. It is certainly curious that after his insistence to be heard, and his declared threats if he were not, Mr Duke appeared not to have prepared what to say. In the event, he moved that the previous order— to convey the new courts to the county with a debt of £807 placed on the rates—be declared invalid. His address was long, and Bruges' reply was longer. Again the arguments were raked over; Duke attacked Ludlow Bruges even more violently than before, and his extravagant rhetoric caused much laughter. He accused Mr Neeld of being merry, to which Neeld responded: 'I confess it is impossible to refrain from laughing. You are so extremely facetious', which caused more laughter. Mr Duke was being mocked, and quite mercilessly. The newspaper report of his speech was littered with 'laughter', 'much laughter', 'general laughter', etc. He commented that he was glad to afford merriment, and it is a measure of the singleness of his purpose that he carried on regardless. And having made a big issue of the opinion of Sir William Follett on the matter, he had to admit that Sir William's opinion was that the present case did *not* fall within existing statutes, although he (Sir William) thought that the statutes would not authorize the charge to the rates. 'Counsel', Mr Duke observed, 'for the sake of modesty … generally gave their opinion in a doubtful manner, though they felt positive as to the correctness of it.' It was hardly a fatal thrust with which to end his long speech.

Mr Ludlow Bruges in reply, said that he regretted that a subject that had been so fully discussed previously was again under discussion. Referring to personal attacks on himself by Mr Duke, and to more cries of 'Hear! Hear!', he said he regretted that the language used was 'completely at variance with the order and decorum which had hitherto characterized the debates'. He accused Mr Duke of being rude and flippant, and criticised the open letter where he suggested that he 'might be put down by clamour', when no-one had received a more patient hearing than him. Referring to Follett's ruling, he observed that Mr Duke had said a lot about bad law, but seemed unable to find it. Mr Ludlow Bruges then said that the only way to avoid Duke's 'most frivolous and vexatious opposition' was to apply to Parliament for a bill to settle the matter once and for all. His words were greeted with loud cries of 'Hear! Hear!'

Having dealt with the issue at hand, Mr Ludlow Bruges could not resist feeding Duke some of his own medicine. Mr Duke, he said, had expressed 'honest indignation' at the order in hand, but appeared to forget some of the orders which had originated with him in his character of visiting justice at the county gaol. Mr Bruges said that when he was on the finance committee, it was 'always considered necessary to keep a sharp look out upon Mr Duke's orders'. He would not have alluded to this, he said, but for the 'liberties Mr Duke had taken'; more cries of 'Hear! Hear!' He said that Mr Duke had 'committed an error of judgement' by incurring some charges on his sole authority, and of recommending other charges which the court refused. Duke denied any error of judgement, whereupon Mr Bruges quoted an example relating to the conveying of convicts. Duke said he had no memory of the event, to which Bruges retorted that Mr Duke 'appeared much more astute upon the order in question, than upon matters where his astuteness was required'. He went on to pour scorn on Duke, interspersed with loud cheers and cries of 'Hear! Hear!' Evidently his brother magistrates were greatly enjoying seeing Mr Duke humiliated. Finally Ludlow Bruges proposed an amendment to Duke's motion; the amendment read:

> An order be made for the adoption of such measure as may be necessary (by application to Parliament or otherwise) to enable the County to accept a conveyance of the new Assize Courts at Devizes, pursuant to the term of an order made at the last Quarter Sessions, and to carry such order fully into execution.

Mr Methuen seconded the motion, and the newspaper reported that it was carried unanimously.

On 11 December 1837, an editorial in the *Salisbury and Winchester Journal* provided a narrative of what had happened since the January sessions. Following the unanimous vote, and probably seeking to avoid the expense of an Act of Parliament, Mr Bruges' committee had taken a second legal opinion, not trusting to that of Sir William Follett, regarding the validity of Mr Duke's objections. Serjeant Merewether* had 'confirmed the opinion of Sir William Follett'. The editorial described what happened next:

> In the early part of the Sessions of Parliament of last year, a Bill was prepared and brought in by the officers of the Crown (without reference to the county) for enlarging the powers of the then existing laws of Shire Halls ... The officers of the Crown were informed of the peculiar situation of this county. The former bill was then withdrawn, and another with more extended powers, was brought in, and passed into an Act ... under the provisions of this new law, it is presumed, that the purchase of the New Courts at Devizes will at length be legally effected.

After all, the county of Wiltshire was to be spared the cost of a special Act of Parliament.

The final act in this extraordinary affair was played out at the Epiphany Quarter Sessions held at Devizes in January 1838. The newspaper report described 'a very full bench of magistrates', no doubt prompted by the twin objectives of ensuring that the question of the new courts was finally settled, as well as seeing Mr Duke thoroughly routed. Mr Ludlow Bruges was in the chair, and requested that other matters be dealt with before the question of the new courts. He then vacated the chair in favour of Mr Estcourt, and Mr Heneage read out the presentment regarding the transfer of ownership of the

---

\*     Merewether was a Serjeant-at-Law—a senior barrister similar to a QC.

new courts. This was seconded by Mr Neeld. The account of the subsequent debate, mainly between Bruges and Duke with some input from Lord Radnor, occupied two columns of the *Devizes and Wiltshire Gazette*. Since all of the old arguments were raked over again, it is sufficient to report an extract from an editorial on the subject in the same newspaper:

> It will be seen, by our report of the proceedings at the Wilts Quarter Sessions, that the subject of conveying the new Assize Courts to the County, again occupied a considerable portion of the time of the magistrates on Tuesday. The Earl Radnor and the Rev. Mr Duke appeared in their old places, pregnant with objections; but those objections only served to call forth another masterly reply from Mr Ludlow Bruges, who utterly demolished every position his lordship took, and drove him into such an "awkward situation", that—although it is rumoured he came from Longford to Devizes for the express purpose of opposing the motion for conveying the courts to the county—he felt obliged to back out.

Mr Duke though did not back out. He was determined to fight to the very end, and the editorial gave him credit for that: 'Mr. Duke ... persisted most manfully. Without a leg to stand on ... he shewed fight to the last ... he died positive game'. The vote was twenty-five in favour, with just Duke and Canon Bouverie against. Mr Duke had not covered himself in glory, in fact it might be said that common sense was a concept entirely alien to him. His objections 'on principle' had cost the county many hundreds of man-hours of fruitless and repetitive debate. His brother magistrates must have been thoroughly sick of the sight and sound of him. But if he was metaphorically dead, he refused to stop moving, or at least writing letters. On 11 January, the *Devizes and Wiltshire Gazette* published a long letter refuting a charge made against him during the Devizes Sessions by Mr Bruges. This referred to Duke's alleged errors of judgement in relation to costs incurred at the county gaol, where he was visiting magistrate. Again, Mr Duke had resorted to an open letter to get his 'correct' version of events before the public.

One more example of Duke's performance as a Wiltshire Justice of the Peace needs to be mentioned, since in a number of ways it anticipated the 1844 enquiry at Amesbury. The Easter Quarter Sessions of 1839, held at Salisbury, included some business relative to the new prison at Devizes. When this was complete, Mr Duke said that he had some questions to ask the prison governor, Mr Haywood. Haywood rented between four and five acres of pasture on which he kept one or two cows and some pigs for use by his family. Mr Duke repeatedly insisted, although Haywood 'solemnly' denied it, that he had told Duke that visiting magistrates had advised him to rent the ground in order to have a vote for the borough. More importantly, Duke accused him of selling milk to the convicts, and feeding his pigs on potatoes and bread stolen from the prison.

Lord Radnor said that if Mr Duke had received information, a committee should be formed to investigate; he did not think that Mr Duke's approach was proper. Mr Duke responded that he had been 'treated very uncourteously by the visiting magistrates of Devizes on a former occasion, or he would have imparted the case to them'. He was evidently still smarting over his treatment during the Devizes Assizes affair. The other magistrates agreed that the charges should be stated in writing before a committee was formed; the prison governor would then be given the opportunity to answer those charges.

Mr Duke said that from the discussion it appeared that he would be branded as a 'false accuser' unless the charges were established. He then revealed that his informant was a prisoner in Fisherton Gaol, the county gaol at Salisbury to which he was visiting magistrate, and that the prisoner concerned had been convicted of a capital offence. Several magistrates, including Mr Ludlow Bruges, were most unhappy with Duke's course of action. Lord Radnor, previously his ally, expressed the general opinion: 'it [is] impossible to entertain charges on such an authority', pointing out that the officer had been in the service of the county for nineteen years. He then moved a resolution stating that Mr Duke had acted 'incautiously', and 'this court does not think it worth while to take any further notice thereof.' The motion was carried.

All of this was reported in the newspapers. Mr Duke seems to have been let off very lightly, considering that he was accusing a senior officer of the county of stealing public property, and this on the sole evidence of a convicted criminal likely to bear a grudge. It was another example of his exceedingly poor judgement, and he was fortunate that there was apparently no comeback, or at least none that was reported in the newspapers. Mr Clark, one of the other magistrates, said that if such insinuations had been made against him, he would insist on their being proved or retracted; Mr Bruges commented that 'if the charges could not be substantiated Mr Duke must take the consequences'. Lord Radnor said that 'some little odium' would fall upon Mr Duke if the charges were not supported.

## *The Amesbury Union*

On Monday 14 September 1835, Colonel Charles Ashe a'Court wrote to the Poor Law Commissioners at Somerset House informing them of his outline for the new Amesbury Union. The Poor Law Amendment Act had received the Royal Assent more than a year earlier, and Colonel a'Court had only just completed his plan. A measure of the labour involved can be deduced from the fact that Wiltshire alone had well over 300 parishes. These needed to be grouped into unions of twenty or more around a town where the union workhouse could be conveniently situated. Amesbury was chosen as the site for the new workhouse and it, together with twenty-two surrounding parishes, formed the Amesbury Union. Details of the new union, including the criteria for applying poor relief before the 1834 Act, are contained in Appendix 2.

Charles a'Court was a retired soldier who had seen active service in Egypt, Spain, and Italy during the Napoleonic war. He married a wealthy heiress in 1815, and was very briefly MP for the family borough of Heytesbury in 1820. A Wiltshire magistrate, he was involved in suppressing the Swing Riots in Wiltshire in 1830, not only 'reading the riot act' in the presence of active disorder, but also giving evidence of previous good character in support of a number of the accused. In November 1834, he was appointed an assistant Poor Law Commissioner with responsibility for Wiltshire and Hampshire, a position he seems to have embraced with great energy and enthusiasm, judging by his extensive correspondence with the Poor Law Commissioners. Colonel a'Court came to be well regarded by the guardians of the Amesbury Union, and was called upon on several occasions to arbitrate between them and Edward Duke as the relationship between them steadily deteriorated.

In his letter on the formation of the Amesbury Union, a'Court commented on the state of feeling in the county regarding the New Poor Laws. This, he said, had recently altered from an almost universal distrust among magistrates, yeomen, shopkeepers, and labourers, to a general acceptance at the time of writing. The change of heart had come about, he said, in spite of the efforts of itinerant ballad singers at races, fairs, and markets, 'detailing in doggerel verse, cases of cruelty and oppression existing only in their own imaginations'. Colonel a'Court attributed the change of feeling to his own 'intimacy with the magistracy, and acquaintance with almost all the yeomanry'. Regarding 'the lower orders', the pamphlet by Rev Thomas Garnier on the new Act 'addressed to the Labouring Classes', he found to be most useful. He further commented that the area of south Wiltshire, where Amesbury was situated, was 'more thoroughly pauperised and demoralised' than any he had yet visited. He cited with apparent incredulity, an instance where a man was supporting himself, his wife, and three children on just six shillings per week from the parish. Cobbett in his *Rural Rides*, had railed against the iniquity of parish allowances in the area. Writing around nine years earlier about labourers' wages in the Avon valley, he was outraged that in a place of such agricultural plenty, married labourers with three children were expected to live on an amount allowed by the parish, that was around a third of what he regarded as a reasonable amount to pay just for food, regardless of all other essentials.

The first meeting of the guardians of the new Amesbury Union was held at the George Inn, Amesbury, on 12 October 1835. Each of the parishes was represented by one guardian, with two for Amesbury on account of its size. There were also three ex officio guardians, as well as Colonel a'Court who represented the Poor Law Commissioners. The ex officio guardians were Sir Alexander Malet, baronet, Rev Gorges Paulin Lowther, and Rev Edward Duke. Malet was a career diplomat who spent most of his time overseas and seems to have taken little part in the affairs of the union. Gorges Paulin Lowther was rector of Orcheston St George, one of the parishes within the Amesbury Union, a post he was to hold for more than 50 years. From the census returns and parish records, together with his French names, it can be deduced that Lowther was born in Lyons in France, and baptized in Clifton, Gloucester. He graduated from St Mary Hall, Oxford, and after spending some time as a curate on the Isle of Wight and then rector at Barton Blount, Derby, he came to Orcheston St George. He was also a prebendary of Salisbury Cathedral and a magistrate.

It was resolved that Rev Gorges Lowther be appointed Chairman of the Guardians, with Robert Hughes as Vice-Chairman, and that Richard Munkhouse Wilson be appointed Clerk to the Union at an annual salary of £50. Wilson, who was twenty-six years old at the time of the meeting, was an attorney at law and a Master Extra at Chancery. An auditor at a salary of £20 would be appointed, and 'Messieurs Brodie' would be requested to act as treasurers. Three relieving officers, one each for three groups of seven or eight parishes, were appointed at annual salaries of between £60 and £70, and in addition to his other duties, Rev Gorges Lowther was appointed relieving officer of the group including his own parish of Orcheston St George. It was decided that subsequent meetings of the guardians would be held at the George Inn every Monday morning, and a committee was appointed to select a site and plan for a workhouse designed for 200 inmates (at Colonel a'Court's suggestion), although this was later reduced to 150 inmates.

The Poor Law Commissioners approved a loan of £3,500 to build the new workhouse, and two years later it was nearly ready for occupation. On Monday 27 March 1837, Charles Ralfs and his wife Amelia, were unanimously elected master and matron; their salary was £80 per year, and included an allowance of coal, candles, and vegetables. Duties included schooling the younger inmates. Since Mr Ralfs was at the centre of the 1844 enquiry, it is appropriate to say something about his background. Charles Ralfs was almost certainly born Charles Ralfs Martell, in 1785 in Portsea, Hampshire. The parish of Portsea, situated on Portsea Island, contains the Portsmouth Naval Dockyard. His parents, Henry Ralfs Martell and Mary Bridger, had been married in Alverstoke on the Gosport side, and may have moved to Portsea to allow Henry to work for the navy in some capacity. It was a time of almost continual war with the French, and it is possible that Henry Martell had experienced some prejudice in Portsmouth due to his French surname. In any event, his son joined the Royal Navy as Charles *Ralfs,* having switched his middle and last names; his naval pension registration named him Charles *Martell* Ralfs.

In 1844, Charles Ralfs made a long statement in which he detailed his service to his country, which must have started at the time of Nelson. He had been a master sail maker at Chatham, Deptford, and 'Upper Canada' (Kingston, Ontario). These were all naval dockyards and, since he was a sail maker, it seems likely that he worked mostly ashore and not on board ship. In one of the communications from Gorges Lowther to the Poor Law Commissioners, Ralfs was described as having been a 'purser on the quarterdeck of a man o' war', although if this were true, it seems probable that he would have mentioned it in his statement. An obituary in 1853 stated that he had served 'many years in Her Majesty's service'. It was, of course, in *His* Majesty's service that he was employed.

The births of his children might throw some light on Ralfs' movements during his time in the Navy. In 1803, he married Amelia Phillips in Portsea; he was eighteen years old, she was about a year older. Their first child, Amelia, did not arrive for eight years and, intriguingly, was born in Guernsey around 1811. Since Trafalgar, the Royal Navy had had mastery of the seas, but the proximity of the French coast to the Channel Islands was an ever-present threat. In October 1811, *The Times* reported a rapid deployment of British troops to Guernsey; this was to repulse an expected attack from 30,000 French troops and several ships that were massing at Cherbourg. Guernsey would, therefore, seem an unlikely choice for a safe haven to have a first baby.* There was no naval dockyard at Guernsey, so Ralfs would not have been stationed on the island. One possible explanation for their presence is that they may have been in transit to Canada, but were forced by inclement weather or contrary winds to find shelter. Possibly also, their ship, en route to Canada, was diverted to Guernsey to carry troops or supplies there. The coming 1812 war with the USA would have prompted a build-up of resources in Kingston, which was where Ralfs spent some time and was where the two younger children were born. The Royal Navy base at Kingston—at the eastern end of Lake Ontario near the St Lawrence River—was very important in that war. Ralfs was a 'Salaried Officer and Foreman', and on his retirement in 1829, he was awarded a pension of £40 per annum.

Charles Ralfs and his family returned to England and he was employed for a while as a relieving officer by the Romsey Union. Romsey was just over twenty miles north-west of Portsmouth and, even though it was in Hampshire, the union included a couple of Wiltshire parishes. It was said later that Colonel a'Court had recommended him for the post at Romsey. In January 1837, the Romsey Union decided to reduce from three to two the number of relieving officers needed, and Ralfs lost his job. It is possible that a'Court, who knew that there was

---

* The name 'Martel' (with one 'l') is quite common in Guernsey so it is possible that there were family ties on the island.

the post of master going at Amesbury, recommended him for the job there.

Notwithstanding Mr Duke's subsequent charges against Charles Ralfs, his time at Amesbury was generally unremarkable. Although part of the Ralfses' duties was to act as schoolteachers to the children in the workhouse, the number of children involved, there were more than sixty, proved too much for them. In 1840, their daughter Amelia Benham, who may have been widowed, was formally employed by the union as a schoolmistress at a salary of £20 per annum. The 1841 census shows their daughter Clara also acting as a schoolmistress at the union.

Charles Ralfs was involved in one potentially very distressing incident which Mr Duke might not have been aware of. In January 1840, Colonel a'Court forwarded a note to the Poor Law Commissioners that he had received from Richard Wilson. It was to apprise him of an incident that had taken place at the workhouse. There had been a burst pipe in the cold weather, and a charcoal brazier had been placed in one of the children's dormitories to dry it out. The brazier was removed from the room, and twenty-nine girls were put to bed with the door open but the windows closed. Half an hour later, the girls were found to be very sick and some insensible. Mr Ralfs and his daughters ran upstairs and applied hot and cold water to the girls to revive them. Although all of them had recovered, the surgeon was sent for as a precaution. Wilson went on to say that although everyone in the workhouse knew what happened, there was no dissatisfaction and no complaint had been made. He added that the persons who had suffered most were Mr Ralfs and his daughters from their exertions.

Some of the guardians were also aware of what had happened, but the matter was not brought before the board 'publickly', perhaps with Mr Duke in mind. No blame attached to Mr Ralfs, but the incident operated as a caution to everyone concerned.

## Reverend Duke and the Amesbury Union

Edward Duke, in his status as a Justice of the Peace, had written to the Poor Law Commissioners on several occasions since the 1834 Act came into force. He was seeking advice on specific cases of poor relief, since the parish officers responsible for administering the relief under the old Poor Laws were appointed by, and answerable to, the magistracy. Any pauper considering that an application for relief had been unfairly refused or insufficiently granted, could appeal to a magistrate. During the transition period between the new Act receiving royal assent, the establishment of the Amesbury Union, and the building of the new workhouse, there was an inevitable period of uncertainty where guidance was needed.

With the establishment of the new union and the election of guardians, correspondence with the commissioners on workhouse business might be expected to be conducted by the union secretary or clerk, Richard Wilson, as 'directed by the guardians'. But in June 1836, Mr Duke recommenced writing to the Poor Law Commission (PLC) on his own account. In nearly every case, his letter contained complaints that the new law was being applied incorrectly within the Amesbury Union, and implied that he had failed to persuade the other guardians of the fact. Sometimes he charged an individual officer of the union, or the workhouse master, or even the clerk of the union with misconduct.

Colonel a'Court, the assistant commissioner with responsibility for Wiltshire, wrote to the commissioners in late September 1836, and his letter explained the situation: 'Mr Duke, an ex officio guardian has, I find, been writing to you'. Duke had been complaining that decisions made by the guardians, and sanctioned by a'Court, were incompatible with the new Act. Colonel a'Court went on: 'Mr Duke is an excellent man but somewhat unpopular'. He opined that Duke was annoyed at not being voted chairman or vice-chairman of the guardians, and also commented that he failed to command a majority on almost any question before the board.

Thus as with the Wiltshire magistracy, so also with the Board of Guardians of the Amesbury Union, Mr Duke seemed to have an unerring ability to foster conflict with his peers. He did this by the simple expedient of refusing to abide by any decision made by a majority vote with which he disagreed. Between June 1836 and April 1844, Duke wrote to the PLC more than seventy times. His complaints ranged from the childishly trivial, to a charge effectively of manslaughter against the workhouse master.

The first major disagreement with the other guardians concerned the case of Samuel Brazier. This dragged on for more than a year, and it is appropriate to examine it in detail in order to illustrate the lengths Mr Duke was willing to go to in order to get his way. In late May 1837, Brazier's wife Ann had become dangerously ill with typhus fever. Samuel Brazier was not a pauper receiving relief, but Mr Duke ordered Charles Pyle, the surgeon of the Amesbury Union, to attend Ann Brazier. Article 54 of the new Act appeared to allow for this in cases of 'sudden and urgent necessity'. Mrs Brazier subsequently died. Certifying her death, Mr Pyle wrote that since Ann Brazier had died from a 'malignant fever', it was necessary to bury her as soon as possible.

On 2 June, Mr Duke wrote a rather sharp letter to Mr Farr, the relieving officer, which was delivered by Samuel Brazier himself. He told Farr that unless he authorized payment for the funeral from the poor rates, he would, on his own authority, instruct the overseer, Mr Pinckney, directly to do so. The tenor of this communication suggests that there had already been some tension between Duke and one or other of the relieving officers over this or similar cases. Subsequently, Lowther confirmed that such a case had recently occurred.

Farr examined Samuel Brazier on his financial resources, and learned that he was paid ten shillings per week as a carter to Mr Grey. Grey, was a tenant of Mr Duke and one of the three ratepayers of Wilsford-cum-Lake.* Brazier had five children, one of whom was a boy earning two shillings and sixpence a week. When Brazier was asked whether paying for his wife's funeral would distress him he said: 'it would straiten me for some weeks'. Farr told him that he could not help him, and wrote a very apologetic letter to Duke saying that he did not regret the position Mr Duke had taken, but that he had had to reject the request from Brazier; he would, however, report the case to the board who would decide the matter.† The guardians met on 5 June, and of the seventeen present, fifteen voted *not* to repay the eighteen shillings to 'the parish officers of Wilsford and Lake', since Samuel Brazier was not a pauper, and not receiving relief from the board; only Mr Duke and one other voted in favour. Seemingly, the payment to Samuel Brazier had already been made. On 9 June, Mr Pinckney wrote a letter to Farr which was delivered by Duke's servant. He informed Farr that he had paid for the funeral 'in consequence of the sudden and urgent necessity of the case', adding that this was 'according to the Poor Law and the direction of the Poor Law Commissioners', which sounded suspiciously like

---

* The parish was also known as 'Wilsford and Lake'

† The new Act seems to have set the poor rate for any parish to be the equivalent of the average rate for the previous three years, and likewise the threshold for relief. For the Amesbury Union, the maximum weekly wage to qualify for relief was between six and seven shillings; since Samuel Brazier's income was considerably above that threshold, Mr Farr was quite correct; Brazier did not qualify for relief under the Act.

words dictated by Mr Duke. It is not difficult to conclude that Duke had instructed Pinckney to make the payment, as he had threatened in his letter to Farr, and then encouraged him to write the letter in order to justify the action.

Finding himself in a substantial minority was a normal circumstance for Mr Duke, so just as he had done with the Wiltshire magistrates when he could not get his way, he retained the services of a barrister to offer a legal opinion on the matter. He sought a judgment from Serjeant-at-Law Henry Merewether, the barrister previously used by the Wiltshire magistrates. Duke may have reflected on the fact that Merewether's bill was probably several times the eighteen shillings paid for the funeral, but from his point of view it was a matter of principle.

Merewether's judgment was delivered on 11 July 1837. He was of the opinion that the case resided outside of the new Act, as a result of which neither the guardians nor the PLC had the ability to 'exercise a judgment' on the matter. He advised the overseer to charge the money to his accounts, suggesting that 'no magistrate will hesitate to allow the item'. This opinion does seem odd, since if the case 'resided outside of the new Act', how could any magistrate called to adjudicate possibly allow an expense which had been specifically justified by Article 43 of the new Act?

Nevertheless, the overseer did as he was advised—encouraged, no doubt, by Mr Duke. When the accounts came to be audited, the auditor, after having been shown Merewether's judgment by Mr Duke, wrote to the PLC asking for guidance since the guardians had already refused the item. Somewhat unhelpfully, the commissioners replied that 'the question is not free of difficulty', and it was necessary to refer to the Board of Guardians. They then wrote to the Board of Guardians asking what they had decided, as well as requesting any further information that might be relevant.

On 30 December 1837, Mr Duke wrote to the commissioners in response. He said that there were great irregularities in the case, and that the decision of the guardians not to allow the charge was illegal, claiming that when he left the meeting, he had been under the impression that the vote by a show of hands had allowed it! He commented that the particular guardian for the parish in question was ill and had not attended a number of meetings. He added a note, signed by all of the ratepayers of Wilsford-cum-Lake, to the effect that they knew Samuel Brazier, that he was an industrious and honest man, and that the cost of his wife's burial should be borne by the parish. The ratepayers of Wilsford-cum-Lake were Mr Duke himself plus two others—one of whom was Samuel Brazier's employer.

Three weeks later, Richard Wilson wrote to the commissioners with the union's version of events. He pointed out that the matter had been discussed frequently, Mr Duke having many times brought it before the board and having taken a legal opinion. Nevertheless, the guardians were quite happy that they had made the correct decision. Furthermore, they considered Mr Duke's letter, a copy of which he had given them, to be irrelevant and impossible to substantiate.

Gorges Lowther, the chairman of the Board of Guardians, clearly felt embarrassed by Mr Duke's behaviour in respect of Samuel Brazier, and the appearance that the Amesbury Guardians were in disaccord. He also wrote to the commissioners with the intention of giving them 'a plain statement of the facts as they appeared to the board, divested of the dramatic character in which they have subsequently been clothed'. Mr Lowther said he had questioned the relieving officer on the case, 'of whom I cannot say less than that he discharges his duty with great zeal, judgement, and humanity', and he had said that he did not think it was 'a case for assistance'. The unfortunate Brazier, as well as his wages and that of his son, had 'market money and Michaelmas pay'.

Lowther said that there had been a very similar case the previous week that had also been rejected by the board. He finished by saying that it would have been wrong to establish the precedent that 'a man with twelve shillings and sixpence weekly wages should be allowed to paupery'. In a postscript, he said that there was appended a formal refutation of the claims made in Mr Duke's letter to the board. Lowther made nine points, of which the main ones were: Brazier was not a pauper, cases were frequently rejected in opposition to the guardian of the parish, and the application had been almost unanimously rejected by the guardians. Finally, he commented that 'this very trumpery grievance' should never have been brought before the Board of Guardians, let alone the Poor Law Commissioners, since the guardians had considered the case on numerous occasions and rejected it accordingly.

Duke wrote again to the commissioners on 27 February, again stating his position on Samuel Brazier; apparently, he received no reply. He wrote again on 2 June on an entirely different subject, requesting a copy of the workhouse rules. This may have been prompted by a meeting of the guardians on the same day; the minute book notes that Mr Duke complained that 'contracting for provisions' for the workhouse was improper, and complained about the 'undue interference and general impropriety of the clerk'. This was followed by a 'unanimous' resolution, surely without Mr Duke's vote, to the effect that Mr Wilson, the clerk, had performed his very able and valuable duties conscientiously and efficiently. Evidently Duke had formed a grudge against Richard Wilson, possibly over the voting in respect of the case of Samuel Brazier.

Mr Duke wrote to the PLC on 13 June, reminding the commissioners that they had yet to answer his previous letters, restating the case of Samuel Brazier in its entirety, but now saying that he and the other two ratepayers of Wilsford-cum-Lake had paid the eighteen shillings due for the funeral. The PLC replied to him a few days later. Apparently a response had been drafted to his earlier letter, but 'owing to accidental circumstances was not sent'. In fact the reply, had it been sent in February, would have been of little use. The commissioners pointed out that their mandate prevented them from ordering relief in individual cases, and were placed in a position of 'some difficulty' when asked to comment on the decisions of boards of guardians. They did think, however, that Samuel Brazier's case was not one of 'sudden and urgent necessity'. But just in case anyone thought that the commissioners had actually made a decision, they added that this view was not 'clothed with any judicial authority', and was not binding on any magistrate or auditor who might have to examine the accounts.

The matter of Samuel Brazier appeared to be settled, no thanks to the PLC, and a considerable amount of trouble had been caused to all concerned. In fairness to the PLC, and Mr Duke may not have really understood this, it was explicitly precluded by Article 15 of the new Act from ordering relief in individual cases. The alternative would have been an inundation of appeals from people who felt they had been unfairly treated by local unions. The executive power in such matters quite properly resided with the local boards of guardians.

In Mr Duke's defence, he was evidently motivated by a charitable disposition towards the less fortunate, and Article 54 of the new Act allowed a Justice of the Peace to authorize medical relief in the case of 'sudden and dangerous illness'. The case of Samuel Brazier highlighted aspects of Mr Duke, the PLC and the Poor Law Amendment Act itself that were to be repeated frequently over the following years. The powers of the PLC were limited to administering, enforcing, and occasionally amending the workhouse rules. Mr Duke was to question 'amendment', while insisting on 'enforcement', time and time again.

In April 1839, Colonel a'Court wrote to the commissioners from London; his letter was headed 'Leave requested for the

Amesbury Guardians to hold fortnightly instead of weekly meetings'. For some time, the guardians had been meeting every two weeks, a fact of which a'Court was fully aware and had approved. He had spoken frequently to the officers of the union and the paupers to assess the proper working of the union under that arrangement. He was 'satisfied that fortnightly meetings ... may safely receive your official sanction'. He said that he knew Mr Duke was about to accuse the clerk of disobedience in respect of not holding weekly meetings, although Duke knew that a'Court was 'fully cognisant of the fact'.

In his campaign against the clerk, Mr Duke had read the rules as laid down by the commissioners. Rule 6 in the section 'Meetings of the Board of Guardians' says: 'The guardians shall meet at least once in every week', although rule 9 says: 'The majority of the guardians present in any weekly meeting may, if necessary, adjourn to the same day of the next meeting ... as they may think fit'.* A week later, Mr Duke did write to the PLC regarding weekly meetings, but primed by Colonel a'Court, the PLC wrote back telling him that 'in various unions fortnightly meetings have been sanctioned by the commissioners.' Furthermore, they pointed out to him that weekly meetings had been 'long discontinued' at Amesbury.

Undeterred, Duke wrote to the commissioners the following week. The Amesbury guardians, he said, only wanted to stay with fortnightly meetings to 'save their own trouble'; their evidence that this was acceptable was ex parte (from one side only) and biased. Mr Duke wrote, he said, as a magistrate with twenty-four years of experience in dealing with the poor. He told them that his two farmer friends, the other ratepayers in his parish, were 'decidedly of his opinion'. He accused the commissioners of having a 'vacillating policy ... I have supported you who have deserted yourselves and me'.

---

\* From the First Annual Report of the Poor Law Commissioners, 1835

If Mr Duke wanted to get the commissioners on his side, he really was going the wrong way about it. He finished his letter by citing the case of a pauper by the name of Lawrence. He appeared to be getting the run-around between the overseer and relieving officer, because a meeting of the guardians was not due for more than a week. Colonel a'Court wrote to the commissioners two days later. He started his letter:

> I never expected that the Revd. Mr Duke's most restless spirit would allow him to remain quiet under his disappointment at not setting aside the order for fortnightly meetings.

Mr Duke had told Colonel a'Court that he 'disputed the right of the commissioners to amend their former "general rule"'. And just as he had done twice before, he said that he intended to get 'counsel's opinion' before proceeding any further. Colonel a'Court pointed out to the PLC that he had visited Amesbury and attended a meeting of the guardians when the whole of the business had occupied no more than two hours. He suggested that the commissioners write back to Duke and tell him that they had referred his letter to the 'assistant commissioner', who was, of course, Colonel a'Court himself. The following month, Richard Wilson wrote to the PLC with an account of what had happened to the pauper Lawrence, finishing by saying: 'This ... does not prove Mr Duke's allegation of the inconvenience of a fortnightly meeting'. The letter was accompanied by a note from a'Court which said: 'it does not appear expedient that any further notice should be taken of the Revd. Mr Duke's statement to you'.

Duke's correspondence with the Poor Law Commissioners now sank to a trickle, but in January 1842, after he had written to them complaining that some relieving officers in the Amesbury Union were admitting many more paupers than others, his simmering resentment against the union boiled over; he wrote to a newspaper on the subject. His letter was published on 11 January, addressed to the editor of *The Sun*, and entitled 'Amesbury Union':

> Sir—I have been informed, on indubitable authority, that some time since a very high panegyric appeared in your newspaper, on the conduct and management of the Amesbury Union and house.
>
> As an *ex-officio* Guardian of that Union, I am intimately acquainted with all its transactions, and must beg leave to contradict any assertion as to its very superior merits. I must honestly undeceive the public by saying, that in its conduct and management I consider it inferior to the majority of Unions in the kingdom.
>
> I am, sir, your obedient servant, Edward Duke, Lake House, Wilts, Jan 7.

The editor had added a note to the bottom: 'Will our correspondent inform us when the panegyric on the Union appeared?'

It is quite difficult to understand what prompted a serving officer of the union, an experienced magistrate, and a very senior member of the community to go public in such a manner; but it was not the first time that Mr Duke had resorted to this type of measure, and it would not be the last. It does suggest that his relationship with the Amesbury Union had effectively broken down. It is also notable that he had rushed into print with faulty intelligence, since clearly the 'panegyric' had not appeared in *The Sun*.

Richard Wilson informed Colonel a'Court (who had either recently resigned as an assistant commissioner, or was just about to) of the letter, and he wrote back saying that he was surprised. Only a month earlier, Duke had written to him saying that following a visit he had every reason to be satisfied with the Amesbury Workhouse, although he approved neither of the mode of outdoor relief, nor of what he considered to be the 'interference of the union clerk [Richard Wilson]' in decisions made by the guardians. Colonel a'Court went on to say that Duke's criticism of the clerk was brought before a very full meeting of the guardians at which a'Court was present. Duke had said that many of the guardians had complained to him privately about the clerk, but at the meeting 'not a single individual would bear out the assertion'. Colonel a'Court then paid tribute to Wilson's excellent service to the union, commenting also that he had never felt the need to question any decision regarding outdoor relief; he finished: 'I request you will submit this communication to the Board of Guardians, it is the only notice which I think ought to be taken of Mr Duke's published letter'.

But Mr Duke was not to be ignored. Perhaps buoyed up by seeing his complaint in print, he wrote to the PLC on 19 January 1842 to press his advantage. He reminded them of his recent communications to them, including, as he put it, 'support[ing] your rule under the enforcement of the law' in respect of the change from weekly to fortnightly meetings. He said he felt hurt that the PLC had not supported him, when he was attempting to support them in the enforcement of their own rules. He went on to say that 'under that hurt' many would have retired from the board, but that was something he would never do. Having lectured the PLC on its own shortcomings, Mr Duke now laid out four specific charges of infringing PLC rules against the Amesbury Union:

1. The eighty or so children in the workhouse were allowed clean stockings only once per fortnight, and none at all in the summer.
2. In the event of the death of a pauper, the medical attendant does not make a special report to the guardians of the death and its causes, 'which for obvious and good reasons you require'.
3. The 'order check book is altogether withdrawn' and 'disadmitted' as useless.

4. The 'pauper description book' is also withdrawn, and 'in like manner dismissed as useless'.

He then repeated what he had said earlier about the PLC not supporting him on the question of weekly meetings, going on to say that other unions had found the change of the rule 'inexpedient and injurious'.

Mr Duke finished by hoping that the PLC would 'resolve to maintain' its rules, so that he would not need to invoke Article 43 of the Poor Law Amendment Act. That section allowed him, as a Justice of the Peace, to perform a formal visit to the Amesbury Workhouse to establish whether the 'rules, orders or regulations' were being observed, and to hand out 'penalties and punishments' if they were not. The PLC acknowledged Mr Duke's earlier letter with five pages of comments, and a short note at the bottom thanking him for the latest intelligence on the 'infringement' of PLC rules.

The commissioners wrote to the Amesbury Union inviting comments, which Richard Wilson responded to on 8 February. He said that since the guardians were not due to meet for some days, he would supply answers 'such as I am able' in the meantime. On the question of stockings, Mr Duke was correct, although the fact that the children were given clean stockings only once per fortnight, was known and approved of by the visiting committee. The reporting of a pauper's death to the board had not been done in the past, but no deaths had occurred in the workhouse for the previous six months, and shortly after the previous death, Wilson had requested the medical officer to provide a report in the future.

The order check book had been discontinued shortly after the formation of the union as providing no check whatsoever. It was resumed in the middle of 1838 after Mr Duke had threatened proceedings against the clerk(!); it was used for around a year until Duke himself admitted its inconvenience, and had not been used since. Wilson went on to detail several examples of that inconvenience. The pauper description book had not been withdrawn, and had been available at least over the previous two and a half years either in the boardroom or the clerk's office.

Wilson wrote again on 15 February; the subsequent meeting of the guardians had 'perfectly concurred' with his answer to the PLC. Not, however, Mr Duke. He wrote to the PLC two days later reiterating his complaints of rule infringement. He wrote again on 7 March, claiming that the methods of buying food and clothing for the workhouse were not open to competitive tender: 'This union is so highly irregular in its management that I do trust you will support me in your rules'. He wrote again on 18 March. On the same day, the PLC wrote to the Amesbury guardians; Mr Duke's barrage of correspondence had forced the commissioners to respond. On the question of clean stockings, they said, 'the master of the workhouse [had], therefore, committed a breach of the commissioners regulations', and should be 'reprimanded for his past neglect'. In future, the guardians were to require 'strict compliance' with the rules on behalf of the medical officer regarding paupers' deaths. Notwithstanding the guardians' reason for discontinuing use of the check book, the PLC failed to see how the accounts could be properly audited without it. The letter finished:

> The Commissioners regret to perceive that there has been much irregularity in the above mentioned respects, in the conduct of the business in the Amesbury Union, and they trust that similar irregularities will not again occur.

Wilson wrote to the PLC on 22 March to report that the guardians, by a vote of eight to one, had agreed not to censure Mr Ralfs. On 23 March, Mr Duke wrote to the PLC telling them that the Amesbury Guardians had refused to obey their order to reprimand the master, and reminded them of his charges as to irregularities in tendering for food and clothing. On 26 March he wrote again with further information.

On 31 March, the commissioners asked Mr Parker, one of their assistant commissioners, to go to Amesbury and investigate. It seems probable that the guardians' refusal to reprimand the master precipitated this action. The PLC also wrote to the Amesbury Union to advise them of Parker's imminent arrival to 'communicate their views'. Henry Walter Parker had been an assistant Poor Law Commissioner since April 1839; he had been a barrister at Gray's Inn, and was 'part owner of the *Morning Chronicle* for many years'. Evidently the commissioners had decided that he should take over from Colonel a'Court with responsibility for Wiltshire. The task of the assistant commissioners had been originally to set up the various Poor Law unions, as Colonel a'Court had done at Amesbury. Now, they represented the Poor Law Commissioners in the field when unions needed hands-on assistance. Parker would act as an impartial chairman in the enquiry into Mr Duke's complaints providing, where necessary, advice and guidance as a proxy for the PLC.

The notice from the PLC of Parker's arrival caused all the pent-up frustration of Rev Gorges Lowther, chairman of the guardians, to boil over. He wrote a sixteen-page letter to the PLC on 8 April, and his letter set out the facts in respect of Edward Duke, the Amesbury Union, and the Poor Law Commissioners. He was clearly very angry. Lowther berated the PLC for its lack of courtesy to him in neither informing him personally of Duke's statements nor, until now, sending an assistant commissioner to see for himself what was going on. He said this would not have happened if Colonel a'Court had still been an assistant commissioner, because the 'very mischievous person who is your correspondent [was] well known to him, [as was] his character and habit of making up grievances'. Colonel a'Court, he said, would have informed the PLC that 'it was not safe to act upon his statements without further investigation'. It was a good point; a'Court would never have allowed matters to deteriorate to the present state, and Mr Duke had appeared to restrain himself in his presence.* Lowther went on to praise the virtues of the cleanliness of the workhouse and its occupants as noted by the recent visit of the Archdeacon of Sarum who, having heard of Mr Duke's complaints, came to see for himself.

Lowther welcomed the imminent arrival of Mr Parker, whom, he said, would be able to judge the state of the workhouse for himself, as well as the credence to be given to the information provided by Mr Duke. He was, though, extremely unhappy with the practice of the PLC providing Duke with his own copy of correspondence that had been addressed to the clerk of the union. He described the clerk reading the correspondence to the meeting, while Mr Duke checked every word against his own copy. This had not been received favourably: 'If you propose in future to conduct the affairs of this Union in this manner ... you will create a feeling of great disgust amongst the Guardians'.

He now turned his fire on Mr Duke. From the inception of the union, Lowther said, Duke had systematically opposed the board. Lowther described him as 'one of those busy meddling and grievance-hunting persons with which most neighbourhoods are afflicted'. Colonel a'Court had been 'loath to neutralize the effect of this opposition', but the worst consequence of this was 'tedious speeches' and motions nearly always failing even to be seconded.

Colonel a'Court had retired, at which point Duke recommenced a 'series of petty complaints, abstractedly true, but in spirit utterly worthless'. Lowther then accused the PLC of issuing censures without checking whether Duke's

---

* Duke's letter-writing to the PLC had almost stopped between 1839 and January 1842. It was early 1842, probably after Colonel a'Court had retired as an assistant Poor Law Commissioner, that Duke denounced the Amesbury Union to *The Sun* newspaper.

allegations were founded on fact. He addressed some of Duke's charges, and detailed a letter Duke had sent to a potential supplier in Salisbury containing a 'deliberate untruth'. And he warned of consequences: if the PLC continued the system of 'ex parte information', i.e. acting on information just from Mr Duke, the union would be thrown into confusion. He made the interesting point that the new system had resulted in little or no saving on the poor rates, but the improved 'moral' behaviour of the labouring poor was a matter of satisfaction to the ratepayers. He said that he hoped that this 'beneficial working of the law', would not be broken down by the PLC countenancing Mr Duke's 'petty and vexatious meddling about trifles and petty matters'. Furthermore, he believed that the meddling stemmed from the personal animosity of Mr Duke towards Richard Wilson, the union clerk, noting that Wilson was 'efficient, steady, and diligent'.

Having reprimanded the PLC on its own method of dealing with Duke's correspondence, Mr Lowther now proceeded to charge him with a serious offence. Mr Duke, having failed to persuade the guardians to allow women employed in the workhouse laundry to have an allowance of beer, said in the hearing of several of the inmates that 'he would refuse to work at all until the beer was allowed, if he was in this place'. This was told to Lowther by one of the inmates. On discussing this with the workhouse master, the latter claimed that 'such a speech was sufficient to cause mutiny throughout the house'. This, Lowther said, was a specimen of the 'discretion, judgement, and temper' of the commissioners' correspondent, and the person from whose statements the PLC called on the guardians to censure their master for effectively obeying their orders.

Rev Lowther apologized for the length of the letter, and answered the four specific charges brought by Mr Duke— effectively repeating what Richard Wilson had already told the PLC. Concluding, he said that he had had no intention of saying anything disrespectful to the commissioners, 'whose orders I have made it my business to obey, to cause to be obeyed, most frequently in the letter and always in principle'. Lowther, who as chairman of the guardians had had to put up with Mr Duke's continual troublemaking, pulled no punches in respect of his opinion both of Duke and the PLC. The situation could not be allowed to continue; Lowther hoped, no doubt, that the visit of Assistant Commissioner Parker would effect a solution.

Mr Parker duly visited the Amesbury Union on 11 April 1842, ostensibly in order to enquire into Mr Duke's complaints but also, quite probably, to investigate Mr Duke himself. He must have been taken aback to discover that the four original charges had grown to more than twenty-five. Initially, Parker was reluctant to deal with more than the initial four complaints, but was apparently persuaded by the Amesbury Guardians, and by Duke himself, that all should be investigated there and then. The charges are listed in full in Appendix 3. It is an illustration of the disordered state of Mr Duke's mind that, of the original four that had precipitated Parker's visit, only one was included in the new list. That one, charge number seven—the withdrawal of the order check book—Duke subsequently withdrew.

There are several accounts of what transpired at the meeting, which commenced at 10 o'clock in the morning and finished at nearly 9 o'clock that evening. Duke wrote to the PLC three days later saying: 'the main points of my charges are decidedly proved'. He detailed once more those charges, albeit with the emphasis changed. He did say that he had had only one day's notice of the meeting, and with more warning could have brought in a witness to confirm the lack of regular changes of the women's gowns. On the question of his own conduct, he deplored the 'division of the union' over which he said he had no control. Given that that division was entirely the construct of Mr Duke, this last comment was more than a little disingenuous. He said that the PLC might have been told that he was 'capricious', in answer to which he said that he had 'acted for twenty-four years as a magistrate with a numerous bench ... without the shadow of variance with any one of them'. Mr Duke's colleagues in the Wiltshire magistracy might have argued with that point. He sought to portray himself as a valiant hero standing against the multitude, 'the united and clamorous voices of the many combined against the one'. He had used just this argument in his dispute with his fellow magistrates over the new assize court at Devizes.

But now he sounded a conciliatory note, saying that if his complaints were acted upon, he would 'unite cordially' to heal the divisions existing between the union and himself, and make a 'strong and sincere effort to produce that desirable end'. He added that he would continue always to attend the union meetings. Three days later Mr Duke wrote again, this time to refute two charges made against him. On the question of 'endeavouring to raise insubordination amongst the inmates', he claimed that in conversation with the mistress, and in respect of the non-allowance of some 'refreshment' to the workers: 'I laughingly but in a low voice added that "I almost wondered they did not strike"'. He claimed that he thought no-one else was there, but admitted that it was subsequently shown that the master's daughter and two paupers had been present. He said that he was 'too strict a disciplinarian' to incite insubordination among the paupers, although: 'Had I thus done, I admit that an application to the Lord Chancellor to be "dismissed from the Commissioners of the Peace" would have been my just due.' There was a second charge, which he thought was made in jest, that he had stolen a rusty spoon from the workhouse. He claimed that he had taken it home to show his family, and subsequently thrown it away as unfit for use. He said that in order to 'expiate [his] sin' he would send a dozen new spoons to the master of the workhouse, adding that he had written to the clerk asking that he copy the letter to the chairman and Mr Parker: 'Explanatory not only of my really good feelings but of the future conduct I shall undeviatingly adopt'.

This all sounded like a moderate mea culpa from Mr Duke, having been found out and promising to do better in future. But just in case he had been too conciliatory, he went on to repeat that his charges had been proved, and reiterated that he wished Mr Parker had given him more notice of the visit. He finished by telling the PLC that 'my cause, gentlemen, is in your hands'. His letter to the Board of Guardians did seem to want to produce a more cordial understanding. However lest anyone be in any doubt, his resignation from the union was utterly out of the question, it being a 'sacred duty ever to attend the meetings of the Board'. He did, though, wish that the 'assistant commissioners had themselves adopted a conduct of more mediational nature'. This was the first indication of Duke's view that Mr Parker had not been entirely non-partisan.

Rev Lowther's view of Mr Duke's indiscretion was somewhat different. He reiterated his charge in a letter to the PLC after the event; he was still very angry with Duke. He said that Duke had denied the main charge during the meeting with Parker 'in terms vehement and profane', saying that it was a joke and was said when no pauper was present—which was proven not to be the case. He referred to Mr Duke's 'degraded and humiliating condition' during the meeting, suggesting that such conduct was a grave offence for a magistrate and the Lord Chancellor ought to be informed. On the general tenor of the meeting, Mr Lowther's view was that 'the enquiry was conducted on the part of the Sub. Commissioner with great patience, excellent temper, and acuteness'. Later on, and after he had submitted his report to the PLC, Parker commented on the conduct of the meeting, saying that 'Mr Duke and one or two of the Guardians expressed themselves towards each other with some degree of warmth', this behaviour, Parker did not allow to continue.

So far, so apparently good. Parker sent forty pages of findings to the PLC on 21 May and ten days later, six weeks after his visit to Amesbury, copies of the formal report from the PLC on the investigation were sent to Richard Wilson at the Amesbury Union, and to Mr Duke at Lake House. After detailing the charges in full, the PLC concluded:

> with the exception of the evidence relative to the omission to purchase articles for the supply of the clothing stores by tender, they find nothing to warrant the imputation upon the Board of Guardians and no proof whatever to support the charges impugning the character of individual guardians and the officers of the board.

The letter went on to examine the significant charges, listing explanations where appropriate—reproduced in Appendix 3. It finished:

> they cannot conclude this communication without expressing their regret that a magistrate and a clergyman should adduce charges of so serious a nature as some of these charges undoubtedly are upon insufficient grounds, and that when visiting the Workhouse, he so far forgot his duty as to use language calculated to impair its discipline.

Mr Duke was being strongly censured for his behaviour. He responded to the PLC on 7 June. He was very annoyed, and from seeming to have been satisfied with Mr Parker's investigation, he now turned on him accusing him of having been complained about by the Bishop of Exeter in the House of Lords. Duke had read in one of the newspapers that the Bishop of Exeter (it was actually Lord Wharncliffe) had criticised Parker as having 'acted wrong', in a circumstance related to the Crediton Workhouse in Devon. Mr Duke repeated that he had only been given one day's notice of the visit. He finished the letter with some observations 'in justice to myself', consisting of comments on all twenty-five of his complaints. He added for good measure another issue where he disagreed with the board on the question of relief to Elizabeth Bryant, of whom more later. And Mr Duke now decided, two months and three letters after the event, that Mr Parker's behaviour towards him on 11 April had not been respectful. He would decline any further meetings with Parker at Amesbury, 'from the improper demeanour and highly offensive language of Mr Parker towards me'. Instead he would send a barrister, Mr Edward Everett, as his representative. Parker would not be allowed to 'inverse the order of things by assuming to himself examinant in chief' in future. Mr Parker, he said, must have assumed him to be ignorant of the laws of evidence.

Mr Duke referred again to his alleged attempt to foster insubordination; he said that it was a 'baseless fabric of an observation'. Two paupers had been called during Parker's visit to give evidence of what they heard Mr Duke say; one, he said, heard nothing, the other just the word "beer", and this was 'tortured into an endeavour to introduce insubordination'. He went on, quoting slightly incorrectly from Horace: 'Well may I say "Parturiunt montes: ridiculus mus nascitur"'* which is usually translated: 'The mountain laboured and brought forth a mouse'. He repeated that the charge was absurd. At the bottom of the letter, he added a note to the effect that he would be in London during the following week, and suggested a meeting; while he 'decidedly decline[d]' to meet Mr Parker at Amesbury, he said he would be 'most ready to do so in your presence.'

The following day Mr Duke wrote yet another letter, this one directed personally to Edwin Chadwick; he had drafted the bulk of the 1834 report on the state of the Old Poor Laws. Chadwick had not been appointed one of the new Poor Law Commissioners due to concerns about his social class, but had grudgingly accepted the post as secretary. Some of the early correspondence between the Amesbury Union and the

---

* The quotation should be: *Parturient montes, nascitur ridiculus mus.*

PLC had been with Chadwick himself. His entry in the *Oxford Dictionary of National Biography* states that his involvement with the Poor Law system effectively ended in 1839, so it is unclear why Mr Duke decided to write to him in 1842. It seems that Chadwick was still concerned with the PLC, since the letter bears its 'received' date-stamp two days later.

Mr Duke started his letter by saying that he had written to the PLC by the same post 'correct[ing] some misapprehensions of the commissioners'. He mentioned the case of Jane Conduit* and one other, and repeated that the charge against him of encouraging insubordination was 'trumpery, absurd and false', thus assuming that Chadwick was aware of any of these matters. He now complained bitterly about Parker, saying that his language and demeanour during the meeting was so offensive that he would not meet him again. Duke also complained that when he left the room, Parker was surrounded by the guardians thanking him for his conduct. Mr Duke's animus towards Parker seemed to increase with every letter. However, the Amesbury Union was beyond the pale; he said that he could write a pamphlet on the union that would 'raise a condemnation from John a Groats to the Lands End'. Instead, he threatened to petition the House of Lords to change the law.

On 11 June, the entire controversy was moved on to a new level by a brief editorial note in the *Salisbury and Wiltshire Herald*:

> AMESURY UNION—For the future, in consequence of an appeal by an ex-officio Guardian to the Poor Law Commissioners, the supplies for Clothing and Shoes are to be thrown open to Tender, in previous Quarterly Advertisements.

How had it appeared in the newspaper? The *Herald* was published in Salisbury where Mr Duke had many contacts. It seems likely that as balm to his wounded pride over the

---

\* Details of her case are contained in item two of Mr Duke's complaints—see Appendix 3.

findings on his complaints, he asked the editor to insert this short piece, notwithstanding the curious grammar, to remind the Amesbury Union that they had been forced to concede at least one of his charges. Ah Mr Duke! You should have consulted your Bible first: Hosea 8:7, 'For they have sown the wind, and they shall reap the whirlwind'. The following issue of the newspaper, published on 18 June, contained a letter from Richard Wilson. After all the Amesbury Union had been through at the hands of Mr Duke, having won not only an almost complete rebuttal of his charges, but also a severe censure of Duke himself, the guardians could not let this slight go unanswered. After some preliminary remarks, Wilson pointed out that the 'recommendation of the Commissioners [in respect of the tenders for clothes] has been made solely on general grounds'. Then:

> But as many unfounded statements of the proceedings of this Board have been circulated by the same person, an extract from the letter of the Poor Law Commissioners will serve to shew their opinion of the numerous other charges contained in the same appeal.

He went on:

> The non-purchase of clothing by Tender was one of *Twenty-five* charges preferred by the Rev. E. Duke impugning the conduct of the Board of Guardians collectively, of individual members of the Board specifically, and of several of the Union Officers

He mentioned that an assistant commissioner had been sent to conduct an enquiry, whereupon:

> Mr. Duke desired to abandon seven of his charges, but was not permitted to do so by the Chairman [Gorges Lowther], who said the Board desired the fullest investigation, in order that the charges reiterated month after month, and year after year, might be proved or disproved, and every allegation be thoroughly sifted.

He described how having completed the enquiry, the assistant commissioner reported to the PLC, and their findings were transmitted to the union in a letter from which he quoted (reproduced again in order to add emphasis to Wilson's closing comments):

> The Commissioners ... find nothing to warrant the imputation on the Board of Guardians, and no proof whatever to support the charges impugning the character of individual Guardians and the officers of the Board.

And the commissioners' conclusion:

> they cannot conclude this communication without expressing their regret that a magistrate and a clergyman should adduce charges of so serious a nature, as some of these charges undoubtedly are, upon insufficient grounds, and that when visiting the workhouse, he should so far forget his duty as to use language calculated to impair its discipline.

Wilson finished the letter by saying:

> In this regret the Guardians participate, and reluctantly, but as a matter of painful duty, consent to this humiliating exposure of an ex-officio member of their own body.

Such an explicit public rebuke as this from the union must have had the sanction of the chairman and a quorate meeting of the Board of Guardians. Years of frustration with Duke's incessant nit-picking had pushed them over the edge, and who could say that they were not justified?

Mr Duke had to respond; his reputation as a gentleman, clergyman, magistrate, and Poor Law guardian had received a full-frontal assault from an unimpeachable source, the PLC, and on his home ground of Salisbury. Naturally, it could not be a short letter, and when it was printed two weeks later on 2 July, it occupied more than one column in the newspaper. The letter was dated 8 June, which was a mistake; it may have been 18 June (the date of publication of Wilson's letter). Mr Duke was prompted in making a response, he said, by the quotation from the PLC which 'involves a serious imputation on my character'. He proceeded to lay bare for public scrutiny all of his own frustrations and actions, his objections, and his feeling that he had been unjustly treated.

Duke wrote that he had 'highly disapproved' of the management of the union, and he declared that it was an *alleged* enquiry into his charges. He repeated the slur on Parker being complained about in the House of Lords. Mr Duke had, he said, had only one day's notice to prepare, and he *withdrew* some of the charges due to pressure of time—he did not retract them. He was disgusted at the superficiality of the enquiry, and the report from the PLC was signed *only* by the secretary, Edwin Chadwick; Duke questioned whether any commissioner other than Sir Edmund Head had seen it. As an example of the ill-management of the Amesbury Union, he cited the case of Jane Conduit in minute detail. He chided the master of the union workhouse for buying shoes from Romsey, twenty-four miles away, when there were good shoemakers in Amesbury, and he mentioned the lack of a weekly supply of stockings for the boys in contravention of the rules. He detailed the charge against him of having sowed dissent, saying that it was baseless. Mr Duke finished by declaring that he would never forsake his duty as a guardian, he regretted the 'injudicious' letter of the clerk (ignoring the fact that he himself had almost certainly initiated the exchange), and declined even reading, let alone responding to, any further communication from that quarter should it appear in the newspaper.

There was no comment in the *Herald* in the following weeks, either to Richard Wilson's letter, or Mr Duke's lengthy response. The *Salisbury and Wiltshire Herald* was a serious newspaper, a broadsheet printed on good quality paper and costing five old pence, the same price as *The Times*, albeit published only weekly, on a Saturday, and containing just four pages. Nevertheless it must have had a substantial readership in the county, otherwise how could the Amesbury

Union have been alerted so quickly to its editorial? Wilson's letter was dated 17 June, six days after the appearance of the editorial, during which time the union must have convened an extraordinary meeting and mandated him to write the letter.

It seems likely that all the newspaper-reading public in and around Amesbury would have been aware of the exchange; the Amesbury Union's dirty washing was well and truly out in the public domain. It is a moot point whether the union or Mr Duke were more damaged by the revelations. From the point of view of the union, they were a relatively new public body subject to scrutiny. The revelation of such disputes and infighting among the guardians within the very heart of the union reflected very poorly on its management.

But it must have been far worse for Mr Duke. He was a public figure, a senior and respected member of the community, a clergyman and magistrate of more than twenty-five years standing and, of course, a guardian of the Poor Law. He had been publicly rebuked, not only by his brother guardians in the Amesbury Union, but by the Poor Law Commissioners themselves, and in his own back yard! It is also questionable whether in 'protesting too much', his long and detailed letter of response did not make matters worse for his reputation.

Meanwhile on 13 June, Parker wrote to the PLC responding to Mr Duke's criticisms of him during the 11 April enquiry. After some preliminary comments, he said that at the end of the meeting Mr Duke had thanked him for the way he had conducted the enquiry, and invited him to dinner and offered to put him up at Lake House the next time he visited Amesbury. He was at a loss, therefore, to understand how Duke might have thought his behaviour and language towards him were offensive.

Mr Duke had mentioned in one of his letters to the commissioners that he would be in London, and it seems that he did have a meeting at the PLC on 16 June with Sir Edmund

Head, one of the commissioners, as well as with Mr Parker. There were no published minutes of that meeting, but what happened may be deduced from subsequent correspondence.

On 20 June, Parker wrote to the PLC with an account of his investigation into Elizabeth Bryant. Duke's letter of 8 June had included a 'solemn declaration' from Mrs Bryant's daughter, Martha Ashman, and her (Martha Ashman's) mother-in-law, stating the circumstances of the case which implied that Mrs Bryant had been ill-used by the system. Parker investigated the allegations and concluded by saying that Elizabeth Bryant was not destitute, and questioned the course Mr Duke had pursued in taking a solemn declaration in an extrajudicial enquiry.

The opprobrium continued to pile on to Mr Duke. On 22 June Richard Wilson wrote to the PLC regarding Duke's statements on Parker's behaviour towards him during the investigation. All the guardians present at the meeting, with the exception of Mr Duke, had corroborated Parker's version of events.

On 25 June, the PLC wrote to Mr Duke. They rejected his objections to Parker's enquiry completely. And it is interesting to note that the draft letter had a section crossed out; referring to the case of Elizabeth Bryant, the deleted phrase said: 'and propose to consider what steps it will be necessary to adopt with regards to your illegal and improper course of proceeding in the matter'. Duke wrote again to the PLC on 27 June, grinding over the same ground and repeating what he had already said on numerous occasions. Referring to the case of Jane Conduit, he cited the opinion of a member of the Corporation of Salisbury in support of his own view. On 1 July he wrote again. This time he said that during the meeting he had had at Somerset House at which Parker was present, the latter had insulted him. Mr Duke also made some new accusations against Parker. He claimed that during the enquiry at Amesbury, Parker had said in front of the other guardians that Duke's complaints were disgraceful, that were he the workhouse master he would bring an action against him, and that he should be 'struck out of the commissions of the peace'. Mr Duke finished his letter by 'praying for the extinction' of the Amesbury Union because of its treatment of him, assisted by the officers of the PLC.

He wrote to Parker on the same day, now referring to the so-called insult at Somerset House when Parker had accused Mr Duke, in front of some PLC clerks, of enquiring into Richard Wilson's private purchases. He also referred to the chairman and guardians crowding around to thank Parker for insulting him after the enquiry at Amesbury, and complained about Wilson's letter in the *Herald*.

On 5 July, Parker drafted a letter to Mr Duke, ostensibly coming from the PLC. Referring to Duke's letter of 27 June, he rejected Duke's comments about Jane Conduit, as well as his comment that his (Duke's) view was endorsed by a member of the corporation, saying that the said person was 'wholly ignorant of the duties of an overseer', and as such 'utterly unworthy of notice'.

Filed close to this letter in the PLC files is a note to Parker from one of the commissioners. It reads:

> Mr Parker, if there are any new facts alleged in Mr Duke's letter, they should, I think, be inquired into—but if not, I do not think it advisable to continue a controversial correspondence with Mr Duke upon points upon which the Commissioners have already expressed their opinion and communicated the same to him.

Quite so. Parker's answer referred only to the case of the unfortunate man with dropsy and that of Jane Conduit, which were the first two of Duke's twenty-five charges. It appears that the letter was sent under the name of Sir Edmund Head, the Poor Law Commissioner with whom Duke had had an interview at Somerset House, and who probably authored the note to Parker, since Duke wrote back to him acknowledging the letter. But if Sir Edmund thought he was going to shut down the correspondence with Mr Duke, he was sadly mistaken. On

6 July, Duke wrote to the PLC: 'On my return into the country I found that Mr Parker had been down to make enquiries as to the death of poor Mrs Bryant.' Mr Duke was convinced that Mrs Bryant had died 'destitute of a shilling', the cause of death being 'a broken heart', and he provided further details of his interaction with her. However, Parker had determined from his visit that she was quite definitely not destitute, so notwithstanding that her death was tragic, she had not qualified for poor relief.

The next day, 7 July, Mr Duke wrote again to Sir Edmund regarding the investigation at Amesbury, and commented on Parker's assertion that he had thanked him for his efforts: 'God is the witness that I write the truth when I write that I never did'. He said he felt grievously insulted by Parker, but 'involuntarily paid a courtesy which ... the instant after I regretted'. He then blamed Parker's report for the 'utterly unmerited stigma on me as a clergyman and a magistrate' resulting from the PLC's censure, based on 'no proof whatsoever'.

The PLC acknowledged receipt of both letters with no comment. It might be expected that the failure of the PLC to more than acknowledge Duke's previous two letters, as well as fallout from his exposure in the *Salisbury and Wiltshire Herald,* would have dampened his enthusiasm. Not a bit of it. Mr Duke was absolutely determined to make the most of his success in forcing shoes and clothing for the union to go to tender. In further correspondence, he demonstrated that the PLC, prompted by Mr Parker, was wrong when it said that no loss had accrued to the union because of the failure to go to tender, because lower terms had been obtained by tender. Nevertheless, as a Christian and a gentleman, Duke forgave 'the insults from Mr Parker', although he could not forget them, and would never meet him 'in conference' again. He proceeded to repeat again his grievances against Parker, and regretted very much that he was not only an assistant commissioner but also the assistant secretary of the PLC. The PLC did not, apparently, acknowledge receipt of this letter.

There followed, from the PLC's viewpoint, a welcome three-month hiatus in Mr Duke's letter writing. Had he taken a holiday? No; in fact he had been delayed by the 'illness of a near relative and other unforeseen circumstances'. But he had not been idle. Perhaps irritated because the PLC were ignoring him, and still smarting from his public rebuke, he decided to redouble his efforts to force them to acknowledge the 'failures', as he saw them, at the Amesbury Union. Mr Duke decided to invoke article 43 of the Poor Law Amendment Act. This allowed the visit of a Justice of the Peace to a workhouse to ascertain whether the rules and regulations were being observed. The visit took place on 10 September; the covering letter was dated 25 October. The report started portentously:

> I Edward Duke, Ex Officio Guardian of the above union (Amesbury) did on the above named day visit the aforesaid union and make my report therein in form and manner following.

This sounded officially legalistic, except that it was a little spoiled by the statement in the covering letter:

> This report is made under the power of the 43rd Sect. of the 76th of 4 & 5 Gul 4. [the Poor Law Amendment Act]. By that act an Ex Officio Guardian is empowered to visit the Union House of his District.

But this is not what the Act says. The Act empowered a *Justice of the Peace* to visit a union house; article 43 said nothing about ex officio guardians. Since Mr Duke was also a JP he still had the authority, but the impact of his communication was a little diminished.

His initial finding was good: 'On a full inspection I found the House to be in general good order and (as is unusual) in the extreme state of cleanliness'. He was generally satisfied with what he found. He made a few minor criticisms, and seemed to be concerned about the quality of the vegetable soup, the peas being hard. However there were 'three glaring and grievous defects' in the Amesbury Union House. So five months after Parker's visit, the rejection of all but one of Mr Duke's then objections, and the newspaper publicity, he started again quite unabashed. His 'new' objections were:

1. The gravel covering of the yard became muddy in wet weather preventing the children from taking their 'healthy exercise'.
2. The lack of a porter.
3. Incoming 'Filthy vagrants' with the 'itch'* were accommodated in the same rooms as other new paupers without the infection.

But surely these complaints had already been dealt with by Mr Parker's investigation? Item one was Mr Duke's previous item eighteen, item two was his previous item ten, and item three was his previous item twenty-four. Mr Duke wrote to the PLC again on 2 November, and once more on 24 November. He cited two instances of pauper on pauper assaults, where a porter would have facilitated the transporting of the paupers to court at Salisbury. Meanwhile, the PLC had sent Duke's latest complaints to the Amesbury Union for explanation without any further comment. Had no-one at Somerset House actually *read* Mr Duke's report? Anyone involved with Parker's investigation should have been familiar with the complaints dealt with in that report, and would have realized that the current complaints had been considered previously and rejected. Furthermore, the PLC had publicly rebuked Mr Duke for his activities at the Amesbury Union—or rather, he had, himself, caused that rebuke to become public. Were the commissioners collectively just not doing their job in failing to intervene in this acrimonious affair? Surely they cannot

---

* The 'itch' was scabies, a contagious skin infestation of the 'itch' mite.

have been unaware of the considerable damage done to the reputation of the union workhouses, and to themselves, by the revelations in the *Salisbury and Wiltshire Herald*?

It might also be wondered how Mr Duke had been appointed an ex officio guardian to the Amesbury Union in the first place, and whether he could, as a considerable and damaging nuisance to all concerned, be removed. He had stated on several occasions that he would never resign. In fact his position was enshrined in the Poor Law Amendment Act itself. Article 38 lays out the rules for the election of guardians for each parish within a union by the ratepayers of that parish. It also states:

> Every Justice of the Peace residing in any such parish, and acting for the county, Riding, or Division in which the same may be situated, shall be an *ex officio* Guardian of such united or common Workhouses ... and after such Board [of guardians] shall be elected ... shall *ex officio* be and be entitled, if he think fit, to act as a Member of such Board

By the Act Mr Duke was entitled, if he wished, to be an ex officio guardian, and could only be removed as such if his appointment as a magistrate were to be revoked. Here then, was the reason that Gorges Lowther had written to the PLC asking whether the Lord Chancellor could not be apprised of Duke's indiscretion vis-à-vis the paupers going on strike for beer. The implication was that he should be dismissed as a magistrate.

Richard Wilson responded to the PLC on Duke's latest complaints on 25 November. His response demonstrates admirable restraint. After acknowledging the communication, Wilson wrote to point out what the PLC ought to have known, that Duke's 'new' complaints had already been dealt with during the Parker enquiry. Nevertheless, he patiently dealt with them again. Mr Duke had highly exaggerated the state of the yards. Money had been spent on them, drainage had been improved, and the children were in excellent health. There was no mandate from the PLC to appoint a porter, the guardians were not inconvenienced by not having one, and until they were one would not be appointed. On the question of vagrants infecting the other residents, Wilson stated that vagrants or other people with the itch were not allowed to associate with the other inmates 'and Mr Duke knows it'. He mentioned 'four detached rooms' added to the workhouse to 'accommodate and keep separate the sick and infirm', adding that 'the general satisfactory state of health of the inmates' was the best evidence of the care taken by the master and medical officer.

Duke had not attended the meeting at which the contents of this letter had been agreed, having been called away to the funeral of his sister-in-law. He did attend a meeting on 28 November, when he was able to read the text of the letter. The next day, he wrote to the PLC. His letter would be brief, he said, although it still occupied four pages. The complaints that Mr Parker investigated were intended to illustrate the 'continuous system of ill-management' of the union, rather than a 'systematic enquiry into each point'. He then reiterated his three complaints, adding that the issue of the receiving room was 'scandalous'. The PLC acknowledged his letters and sent him a copy of Richard Wilson's response. On 9 December he wrote yet again repeating his complaints. His letter was acknowledged on 21 December with no further comment.

But Mr Duke was not to be put off by being ignored. After a few days spent celebrating Christmas, he took up his pen on 29 December and wrote two letters, one addressed to the PLC, and one addressed personally to Sir Edmund Head, one of the three Poor Law Commissioners. To the PLC he noted its mere acknowledgement of his previous letters, saying that a rumour had reached his ears that no notice would be taken by the PLC of any of his letters in future. He said he would be doing the PLC a great injustice were he to believe it, being 'highly detrimental to the cause of public justice', as well as 'so derogatory to yourselves ... insulting to me', and 'so subversive of the laws of the country'. Yet again, he reiterated his complaints, accused the commissioners of failing to investigate by asking the right questions, and for good measure informed them that there was an outbreak of measles in the workhouse.

Duke's letter to Sir Edmund Head—whom he had met when he visited Somerset House—referred to the rumour, repeated his complaints, and called Sir Edmund's attention to his report. He said that it was sent to him because Duke thought he had a special responsibility for the West of England. But it seemed that Sir Edmund too had had enough of Mr Duke. His acknowledgement stated that Duke's letter would be considered by the commissioners, adding slightly condescendingly:

> I think it right to remove an erroneous impression which appears to exist in your mind as to peculiar districts being under the special superintendence of one or other of the commissioners.

On 5 January 1843, the PLC wrote to Duke saying that immediate attention would be given to the 'subjects adverted to' in his letter to Sir Edmund Head. This 'immediate attention', consisted of a copy of Duke's letter being sent to Mr Parker asking him for his observations, and an instruction to him to take such steps as he thought fit. The PLC also wrote to Richard Wilson asking for the medical officer's report on the state of health of the inmates. Duke acknowledged Sir Edmund Head's letter on 6 January, taking more than a page to explain, apologetically, his 'erroneous impression'. He mentioned the measles outbreak, and described the disposition of the reception rooms in detail.

Richard Wilson responded on 14 January with a report from Charles Pyle, the medical officer of the union. Three children had died in the measles outbreak which affected forty inmates, but most were improving. There were also nine cases of 'bilious fever' and four of 'the itch'. Pyle noted that it was the most unhealthy time of the year, and 'the most unfavourable season for some years'.

It is appropriate at this point to take stock and consider the behaviour of the PLC in respect of Mr Duke, and even whether the original Act of Parliament was faulty in respect of the status of ex officio guardians. The three commissioners at the PLC were appointed by government every five years, the guardians in the various unions were elected by the ratepayers once per year, and the paid officers of the union were appointed by the guardians as appropriate. Only the ex officio guardians owed their status purely to the fact that they were magistrates and resident within the union. A rogue ex officio guardian could only be removed, therefore, by revoking his status as a Justice of the Peace. Being a bloody nuisance was hardly grounds for defrocking a magistrate.

But it is also easy to see that no-one at the PLC was taking the trouble to read and absorb Mr Duke's correspondence. Perhaps they were over fatigued with the seemingly never-ending and repetitive stream of letters from him, and it is possible to sympathise with that point of view. But the very reason for the existence of the Poor Law Commissioners was to ensure the smooth running of the various unions, the efficient performance of their guardians and officers, and the well-being of the paupers. Anyone reading Duke's communications, notwithstanding the regular refutations from Richard Wilson, and with knowledge of the outcome of Parker's 1842 enquiry, could not fail to see that something was seriously amiss at the Amesbury Union. The commissioners did nothing other than pass Duke's relentless correspondence either to Parker, whose relationship with Duke was irretrievably broken, or back to the union itself. This highly unsatisfactory situation was allowed to continue, Mr Duke seeming to have an inexhaustible supply of ink and paper, as well as plenty of time on his hands.

Duke wrote to the PLC on 18 January, he commented on the health of the inmates at Amesbury, and reminded the commissioners that they had yet to respond to his latest complaints. Three days later, he wrote again. After some comments about the health benefits of heating the workhouse chapel, he accused the PLC of 'extreme reluctance' in dealing with his correspondence, and failing to pay the 'immediate attention' to it which it had said it would do. The PLC was not behaving towards him, he said, with the conduct that was due to him as a gentleman.

Then he raised the game, challenging the commissioners either to respond to the issues he raised, or tell him that they would henceforth ignore him, in which case he would consider his options. He repeated yet again, that he would never 'withdraw his attention' from the Amesbury Union, no matter what the 'bitter' circumstances or however 'unsupported or forsaken' he was by the PLC. This somewhat melodramatic communication elicited the response that his complaints had been referred to the assistant commissioner for the district. He would deal with them when he visited Amesbury. Since the assistant commissioner in question was Mr Parker, and Duke had already declared that he would not meet him again, this was not what he wanted to hear. Duke wrote again on 4 February, although this letter is missing from the files. From the PLC's acknowledgement, he appears to have referred to his previous letters and wanted some action; he was assured that the commissioners would consider them. Nevertheless, the report containing his latest complaints had been sent on 25 October, more than three months previously; it seemed as though someone was dragging their feet.

Mr Duke decided to raise the stakes further. He told the commissioners that he was glad that they were considering his complaints, as he was about to send a report to the Secretary of State and ask for a special commission of enquiry. He wanted, he said, impartial justice; each point had to be investigated, but not by Mr Parker. If the PLC should choose Parker, then Duke would immediately turn to the minister. He suspected a conspiracy against him from the 'intimacy of Mr Parker and the clerk of the union,' and had heard a rumour about an 'under current setting in against [him]'. He reiterated that he would have nothing to do with Parker. He provided a synopsis of his complaints; this included some that had been dealt with in the April investigation, together with a few new ones:

1. Lack of a hearse.

2. No name or any other 'monument' is allowed to be added to the coffin of a pauper.

3. The receiving room is used for vagrants as well as paupers.

4. The state of the yards.

5. The want of a porter.

6. The bad state of the sewerage.

7. The want of a stove to provide heating in the chapel.

8. The want of a stove or fireplace in the hall where the old and infirm are obliged to wait for a hearing.

The commissioners acknowledged the letter the following day, and were quite firm in their position; they saw no reason to withdraw their confidence from Mr Parker, nor to exempt the Amesbury Union from his responsibility. The PLC also wrote to the Amesbury Union with a copy of Duke's latest complaints, and requested a report from the medical officer in respect of them.

On 15 February, Mr Duke replied. He had never asked the PLC to dismiss Mr Parker nor exclude him from Amesbury, but Parker had insulted him and if he came into the committee room, Duke would leave. Nevertheless, his complaints were five months old and nothing had been done. Mr Duke felt that he was being trifled with and ill-used but: 'I will not yield in the endeavour to obtain justice for the Public and the unfortunate Paupers'. And so on. The letter was acknowledged with no comment.

And now Mr Duke found yet another objection to get his teeth into. Richard Wilson had put himself forward as a candidate for county coroner. Naturally Duke objected; Wilson already had three jobs—Salisbury Coroner, under-secretary at the Savings Bank, and clerk to the Amesbury Union. Another post, Duke said, would prejudice his ability to fulfil his duties in the union.

On 22 February, Wilson wrote to the PLC enclosing a letter from Mr Pyle, the medical officer at the union, which had been requested in consequence of some of Mr Duke's complaints. Richard Wilson commented: 'No complaints of the matters adverted to ... have ever been made to or by any member of the board but himself.' Duke had complained that the two infirm wards, which were originally workrooms, were very near the privies, and the smell emanating from them had prejudiced the health of the inmates. By referring to the minutes of the guardians' meetings at the time, it appeared that Duke himself had moved that one of those very rooms be converted for use as an infirmary. Pyle's letter disputed Duke's claim that potentially infected vagrants shared the receiving wards with other paupers, and said that the privies and general sewerage arrangements although not smelling 'sweet', were in good order and did not prejudice health. He also commented:

> I never saw any private house cleaner than the Amesbury Union Workhouse and I do not believe it possible for any to be kept cleaner, a circumstance which is remarked by every visitor.

Duke wrote again on 24 February. He repeated his objections to Parker, and reminded the PLC that he was 'almost' the senior magistrate in Wiltshire, a Christian, and a gentleman. He also complained again about the privies. The following day he wrote to the commissioners twice. The first letter informed them of the date of the election for county coroner, and repeated his objections to Richard Wilson's candidature. The second letter reiterated, yet again, all of his objections to Parker, pointed out that his previous complaints had still not been answered, and suggested that his communications were not reaching the 'Chief Commissioners'.

On 27 February, the PLC wrote to the Amesbury Union wanting to know whether Richard Wilson's election as county coroner would interfere with his duties as clerk to the union. Duke wrote to the PLC on 1 March reiterating his objections to Wilson's candidature. Wilson wrote to the commissioners on the same day from 'Dick's Coffee House, Temple Bar'. He confirmed that he was a candidate for county coroner for Wiltshire, but was unable to get the endorsement of the guardians of the union to his candidature, since they were not due to meet before the election. This statement would, he hoped, satisfy the commissioners. The Amesbury Union was, he said, a small one, and he had only been absent from meetings of the guardians when prevented by illness. He took the opportunity for a very substantial swipe at Mr Duke:

> So far from the guardians considering that my appointment as Coroner would be likely to interfere with the proper performance of my duties as their clerk, I have received the most strenuous support from every member of the board and from their connections with the exception of the Revd. Edward Duke, who has for the last five years persecuted me in every possible way, and who continually brought complaints against me which I am not aware that he has succeeded in substantiating in any instance.

He had, he said, letters of support from the chairman, vice-chairman, and five of the guardians, as well as from Sir Edmund Antrobus, another ex officio guardian. It was, he said, impossible to calculate accurately the number of inquests that he would be involved with. He went on to say that if his duties should prove to be incompatible with his occupation as clerk of the union, it would be easy to remove him, 'should I refuse to resign which cannot be conceived a very probable course of proceeding on my part'. The commissioners replied that although there were 'objections' to Wilson holding both offices, he would not be required to resign as clerk to the union were he to be elected as coroner for the county.

On 3 March Mr Duke wrote to the commissioners; he had received their approval of Wilson's candidature as well as a letter from Mr Parker. The latter is not in the files, but it is possible to deduce what it contained from Duke's letter and Parker's subsequent communication to the PLC. Clearly, the PLC did not understand with whom they were dealing. Mr Duke decided to put them straight:

> I am, gentlemen, the representative of one of the oldest families in this county. I am a gentleman by birth and education and have acted extensively as a magistrate for this thirty years. I am nearly the senior magistrate of the county.

Parker, he said, had made it impossible for them to meet: 'If he enters the room I shall immediately leave it'. And again Mr Duke referred to a conspiracy: 'It has "oozed out", gentlemen, that my communications were to be received and acknowledged, but not attended to', which was probably true. The last enquiry Parker had conducted was, Duke said, not a proper inquiry. Parker had not followed the rules of evidence, and Mr Duke would not meet him again. He said he had addressed a letter by the same post to the Secretary of State asking him to suppress Parker's inquiry and appoint a special commissioner. He had also retained the services of a counsel. Mr Duke now expressed his astonishment that the PLC had refused to veto the appointment of Richard Wilson as county coroner, and suggested that the case would be brought forward by the Home Secretary in the House of Commons.

In spite of the threats, the files contain no copy of any letter sent to the Secretary of State or any subsequent reference to any such letter. On 10 March, Parker wrote to the PLC with copies of correspondence that had previously passed between himself and Duke. He said that the relationship had completely broken down, and that it was pointless for him to conduct an enquiry into Mr Duke's complaints. On that point at least, he and Duke were at one.

On 14 March, Edwin Chadwick wrote to Mr Duke from the Poor Law Commission in reply to his letter. He said that he was unaware of anything that had passed between Parker and Duke which would preclude Parker from conducting the enquiry, so the commissioners were not justified in asking for the appointment of a special assistant commissioner.

After a brief letter on 16 March, Mr Duke took up his pen in earnest on 22 March. Once more he reiterated his objections to Mr Parker. During the investigation at Amesbury, Parker had allowed the clerk of the union 'without restraint to pour out a volley of personal abuse against me'. Once more he refused to meet Mr Parker, once more he reminded them that he was an educated gentleman and a magistrate of thirty years' experience, and once more he threatened to lay his grievances before the Secretary of State. And having said again and again that he would not sit down with Mr Parker, he now said that he would do so if the PLC would agree to him using a barrister to conduct the investigation. The PLC replied on 31 March that the investigation must be carried out by the assistant commissioner, that is Parker, and questions put to witnesses must be by him, although Mr Duke could use a barrister, and he would be able to question the witnesses if he wished. The commissioners then wrote to Parker with a copy of Duke's letter, and for good measure included the latest list of his complaints. Mr Duke was busy with his magisterial duties for several days, but on 11 April he wrote a rather curious letter to the PLC; he appeared to claim that no counsel would accept a brief on the basis of their proposed enquiry, and he would, therefore, suspend further proceedings for the time being.

So the white heat of Mr Duke's determination to push his case forward seemed to be more than a little tempered. Had someone had a quiet word with him? Why had he not carried through his threat to invoke the Secretary of State? Something had definitely happened. Given subsequent events, it seems quite likely that he was ill. He frequently repeated himself in his letters, and the righteous indignation he was feeling, added to his clear paranoia, must have taken a toll on his health. The commissioners responded on 4 May; they repeated that they refused to consent to an enquiry being conducted on any but the terms which they had already stated.

There now followed an almost unprecedented calm that lasted for more than eight months. Between May and December of 1843, not a single letter was written by Mr Duke to the PLC. He said later, that he had had three attacks of paralysis and wished to avoid 'exciting his mind'. But by late January 1844 he appeared to have recovered, and the ceasefire ended with a jolt. Duke wrote to Richard Wilson with a copy to the PLC. He wanted three items to be tabled for discussion at the next board meeting, two related to paupers, the third, the question of a porter. On the note to Wilson he added a PS to the effect that if the PLC wrote to the union asking questions, Wilson should not respond until the board had approved such a response, rather than responding and receiving retrospective approval. Mr Duke was back with a vengeance. What is interesting though, is that with the exception of a porter, he appeared to have forgotten about his previous complaints. He wrote again on 11 February to announce that, at last, and following his resolution, the guardians had agreed to appoint a porter, although he complained once more about the conduct of the clerk.

There were other letters and other minor complaints over the next few weeks, but on 6 April 1844, Mr Duke finally deployed his doomsday weapon. He addressed a letter to the Home Secretary, Sir James Graham, with a brand new and most serious complaint. He charged that the master of the Amesbury Union Workhouse had mistreated a crippled orphan boy, George Wheeler, when the latter had refused to get out of bed. He had seized him by an arm and leg, thrown him on the hard floor, and then back on the bed whence he cut his head badly against the flint wall. A few weeks later, the boy died.

This charge could not be ignored; Mr Duke had effectively accused the workhouse master of manslaughter. He had started a process which very soon accelerated out of his control. At last he had made those persons he regarded as treating him with contempt sit up and take notice. But he had grasped a tiger by the tail, and would have to take the consequences.

## Reverend Duke and the Amesbury Oliver

S ir James Graham had been Robert Peel's Home Secretary since 1841, and was described as his 'close confidant'; however he faced 'social unrest, Chartism, the emergence of the "condition of England" problem, and a campaign in Ireland for the repeal of the Union'.[*]

It is impossible to know what Sir James made of Edward Duke's letter, but he had far weightier things on his mind; it was forwarded by Mr S M Phillipps, Permanent Under-Secretary for Home Affairs, to the PLC for investigation. Mr Duke had written that he had enquired into the conduct of the master of the Amesbury workhouse, having suspected him of 'maltreating and improperly chastising' the paupers, particularly the children. He now sought a formal commission of enquiry into an incident, which if proved to have occurred, would lead to the master being dismissed:

> In the month of April 1840 there was in the Amesbury Workhouse a poor orphan boy of the name of George Wheeler—he was in the infirm ward and was I believe suffering from scrofula. One day the master came in and ordered him to get out of bed—the boy answered that from his illness he could not—the master repeated his command and on the boy's reiterating his assurance that he was unable, the master seized him by one leg and arm and threw him on the hard brick floor—he then violently seized him again and flung him about the bed striking his head against the flint wall. A few weeks subsequently the boy died, whether from the injuries exceeded by his brutal treatment I cannot say, but I

---

[*] From his entry in the *Oxford Dictionary of National Biography.*

think it highly probable as the boy said at the time, that he felt it would be his death and fresh symptoms (unconnected with his former complaint) immediately appeared, which were sufficient to cause death.

Attached to Duke's letter was a statement from James Fry, a pauper of Idmiston, who was present when the alleged assault took place. The PLC instructed Henry Parker to initiate an investigation without delay, and wrote back to Mr Phillipps to assure him that immediate action would be taken, and he would be apprised of the results. On 15 April, Mr Duke added two more charges against the master; he alleged that he had beaten a boy named Player with a doubled rope so hard that he badly gashed his head. Also, that he had beaten two ten-year-old girls, Sainsbury and Holmes, with a doubled rope and had not entered it into the punishment book. These charges, made to the Board of Guardians, were transmitted the next day to the PLC by Richard Wilson. In reference to the case of the boy Wheeler, Wilson reproduced an entry from the minute book dated 4 May 1840:

A complaint having been made of alleged illtreatment of George Wheeler (a pauper belonging to Figheldean who had died recently) by the Governor of the Workhouse, it was inquired into and found to be entirely without foundation.

He went on to say that the guardians had no information about the other charges other than that supplied by Mr Duke, and added:

The Governor of the Workhouse is aware of the charges but has not been called upon by the board to make any statement upon the subject of them. The board think it fair that in accusations of so serious a nature he should have the benefit of legal advice.

Furthermore,

The board has not thought it necessary to suspend the Governor from the exercise of his duties or indeed to take any other measures than simply to transmit a copy of the charges to the Commissioners.

This was the clearest possible demonstration by the Board of Guardians of their complete faith and confidence in the master, Mr Ralfs, and by inference their utter contempt for Mr Duke and his latest charges. Surely it must have been unprecedented for a man accused of causing the death of a crippled boy, to be allowed to continue the day-to-day care of children? But questions relating to George Wheeler's death and Ralfs' involvement had been considered four years previously, as proved by reference to the minute book. Given Mr Duke's track record of grievance-hunting, the guardians' attitude and behaviour were not surprising.

There was a slight lightening of the mood in a further exchange between the PLC and Richard Wilson when the latter wrote on 18 April. Duke had complained to the PLC about a 'contagious' head condition that some of the children in the workhouse were suffering from, and was in conflict with the medical officer on the subject. Wilson:

> Mr Duke assumes that these children have a "highly infectious" or contagious complaint. The medical officer is at variance with him upon this point and the Guardians prefer his judgement to that of Mr Duke's, backed as it is by the fact ... Every explanation has been made to Mr Duke by the Board and by the medical officer but in vain; he is right and everybody else is wrong.

Here was proof, if it were needed, of the weariness of the Board of Guardians with Mr Duke, and this mood cannot but have coloured their attitude to his charges of cruelty against the workhouse master.

There followed a flurry of correspondence leading up to the enquiry that Mr Duke had yearned for. And now that he had the ear of the Home Secretary, he dismissed the PLC. On 19 April he wrote:

> Mr Duke presents his compliments to the Poor Law
> Commissioners ... He feels that he has been sadly trifled with
> and insulted and no longer seeks justice from them.

He continued, referring to himself in the third person:

> He informs them (of what they ought to have known before)
> that he is a Gentleman and did expect from high Functionaries
> the conduct due to a Gentleman. He will now appeal to the
> Public and under the sanction of the Public Voice he will
> obtain that justice denied by the Poor Law Commissioners.

He was convinced that he would get a special commissioner.
He declared that he hereby closed all correspondence with
the commissioners, and desired that they would not write to
him again. Mr Duke seemed to be happy to have burned his
boats with the PLC, although given what the commissioners
had previously said, he was unlikely to get his special
commissioner. He had also said that he would conduct the case
himself, dispensing with the services of a barrister. Since he
was a magistrate of nearly thirty years' experience, he should
have been capable of doing so.

A fourth charge was added to the existing three against
the workhouse master, that of holding a seventy-five year
old woman for twenty-four hours on bread and water in the
'blind house', a punishment cell, with no 'chair, stool, bed, or
even straw'. Wilson wrote to the commissioners informing
them of this, adding only that the woman in question, Mary
King, was violent and abusive, and had been brought before
the guardians on at least two occasions.

On April 22, Wilson wrote to Duke to inform him that
the PLC had instructed Parker to investigate his charges. Duke
wrote back the same day saying that he would not meet Parker,
repeating yet again that he had no confidence in him, and that
he had 'grossly insulted him'. On the same day the medical
officer, Charles Pyle, wrote an urgent letter, probably to Gorges
Lowther, urging him to contact Parker immediately and get the

enquiry started. He was with Mr and Mrs Ralfs who were in a 'highly excited and nervous state', the consequences of which he could not judge. He added that Duke had again been to the workhouse to interview one of the paupers about the death of George Wheeler.

On 23 April, Mr Duke wrote again to the Home Office. There was no addressee, but from the comment about the legislature, it was almost certainly Sir James Graham. He enclosed the letter from Wilson regarding Parker's visit, and repeated his determination not to meet him. He reiterated all the injuries and insults he had received from Mr Parker— including the supposed comment from the Bishop of Exeter. He declared: 'you can ... incarcerate me but I never will attend to the summons of that indiscreet young man'. He would not, he said, 'submit to the Somerset House anomalous mode of examination'. He said: 'I demand and I will never cease to demand until I obtain it a full and fair enquiry'. Was Mr Duke not being a little indiscreet himself? Making demands of the Home Secretary and volunteering himself to be imprisoned? He added a postscript to the effect that attempts were being made to 'smuggle up this very serious affair', and two principal witnesses were confined to their beds.

The next day Mr Duke received a letter from Parker asking him for a list of witnesses. Summonses needed to be issued, in order to compel them to attend an enquiry to be held by him under 'the direction of the Home Secretary and the Poor Law Commissioners'. Duke wrote back the same day, refusing to supply him with details of any witnesses, and repeating all of his objections to Parker. He did say though, that he had twice tried to get hold of the rope alleged to have been used to chastise the boys and girls, but had both times been refused, firstly by the chairman, Gorges Lowther, and then by the master.

On 26 April, Duke wrote again to Sir James Graham, enclosing the correspondence he had had with Parker, and again threatened to face a fine or gaol rather than attend his enquiry. In a postscript, he added that one of his witnesses had absconded. On the same day, Parker addressed a further letter to him, and now his patience had become exhausted. He advised Duke of the poor health of Mr and Mrs Ralfs, saying that it was the opinion of the medical officer that any delay to the enquiry would have serious consequences for them. He had arranged for the enquiry to take place at the union workhouse on the following Monday, and witnesses would be present. He said that it would be impossible to hold the enquiry in Duke's absence, and regretted, therefore, issuing a summons for him to attend.

Mr Duke's bluff had been called. Would he maintain his stand, refuse to obey the summons, and go to prison until he got a 'full and fair enquiry'? Or would family, medical advice, or just plain common sense prevail? Mr Duke had recently been ill; there was the eight-month hiatus in his letter-writing between May and December 1843. When it actually came to it, he might not feel that at the age of sixty-five, and given the state of his health, he could face the prospect of being locked up. To make matters worse, he was the visiting magistrate at the very same prison in which he would likely be incarcerated. Probably the most telling reason for Mr Duke not to defy the summons, was that if he did so he would place himself in contempt of court, and having committed such an offence, he could not possibly avoid being struck off as a magistrate. Such a proceeding would be humiliating in the extreme, and an unendurable blow to Mr Duke's self-esteem. As well as that, if he was really serious in his campaign to get justice for the paupers in the Amesbury Union, once he was no longer a magistrate his tenure as an ex officio guardian would be at an end. He would then be neither allowed to attend meetings of the board, nor, as at present under the new Act, be able officially to visit the workhouse for purposes of inspection (or interference). So in spite of everything he had said, his apocalyptic threats and the opprobrium he had piled on to Mr Parker, he obeyed the summons, attended the enquiry, met Mr Parker, and gave his evidence.

The hearing took place between 29 April and 2 May 1844, Henry Walter Parker presiding. Parker was a barrister, a member of Gray's Inn—called to the bar in 1832 and, as Mr Duke had noted, also assistant secretary to the PLC as well as an assistant Poor Law Commissioner. He was, therefore, eminently qualified to carry out what was effectively a judicial enquiry into the very serious charges made against the master of the Amesbury Union Workhouse. Parker called forty-six witnesses to give evidence; these consisted of Mr Duke, who also made depositions of his charges, four guardians of the Amesbury Union, the medical officer, the chaplain, the clerk of the union, and many current and past inmates of the workhouse. Neither Mr Ralfs nor his wife was called. This was in line with the standard court procedure of the time known as the Incompetency Rule. This rule, the doctrine of 'incompetency through interest', prevented 'any person regarded as having an interest in the outcome of the proceedings' from giving evidence. There was also the view that the rule prevented the accused from incriminating himself. Counsel for the defendant could cross-examine prosecution witnesses. In default of the accused being unable to speak in his own defence, the accused could, after all the prosecution evidence had been presented, make an unsworn statement. This is what Mr Ralfs did; his statement, not sworn, but starting '[I] do solemnly and sincerely declare', was made before Richard Wilson on 21 May. Why it was made three weeks after the enquiry had finished, might be explained by the time Parker had needed to read, absorb, and report on the enquiry evidence. He sent a complete copy of the evidence to the PLC on 16 May. Almost certainly Ralfs had sight of this evidence, since in his own statement made five days later, he presented a detailed defence against some of the assertions in the witness statements. It is unlikely that he was present at the enquiry since, if he had been, he would not have waited three weeks before making his own declaration. It is also probable that he was excluded in order to avoid any possible objection to him intimidating or influencing the pauper witnesses.

Mr Ralfs' interests were represented by an attorney—unanimously agreed by the guardians to be retained at the expense of the Amesbury Union. He was Mr John Swayne, Clerk of the Peace for the County of Wiltshire. He acted as a sort of defence counsel, cross-examining witnesses on Mr Ralfs' behalf. Duke had claimed that he would retain the services of a barrister to act as a 'prosecution' counsel. Then he had said in a letter to the commissioners that he could not expect counsel to take his case on the conditions set by them. It is far from clear what he meant by that. He had on at least two previous occasions retained the services of a barrister. It is pure speculation, but it is possible that he had made himself a sufficient nuisance to the legal profession also, such that they refused to act for him.

In the event Mr Duke did get some assistance, but from a member of his family. In Parker's report, he wrote: 'Revd Duke assisted by his son, Mr Rashleigh Duke, examined witnesses in support of the charges'. Robert Rashleigh Duke was Mr Duke's third son and, like his two elder brothers, he was to become a clergyman. He was twenty-six years old at the time of the enquiry, and although he matriculated at Exeter College, Oxford, in 1836, he did not graduate BA for another thirteen years, and then from a different college. There is no evidence that he had any legal training. He may either have been there to assist his father, who could have been suffering from hearing difficulties or some other infirmity, or simply for moral support. Since Edward Duke was frequently referred to as 'Mr' rather than 'Rev', and Parker's handwriting was so poor as to make 'Mr' and 'Rev' frequently indistinguishable, it is far from clear when it was Edward Duke or his son doing the cross-examinations. Edward Duke certainly made the initial depositions, but in the text of the witness statements, he was always referred to in the third person. It is difficult to say whether it was him or his son who questioned the witnesses.

The only other person known to be present for the four days other than Parker, the Dukes, and Swayne, was the workhouse chaplain, Rev Fowle. It seems quite likely though, that some of the guardians were also present to witness the proceedings. Mr Duke had refused to supply Parker with his list of witnesses to allow summonses to be issued, but Richard Wilson had provided him with some names, as far as he knew them, so the key witnesses were available on the first day.

The record of Mr Parker's enquiry consists of around 100 pages of foolscap written in his own fairly challenging handwriting, complete with his personal brand of the abbreviation of some words. The majority of the depositions and witness statements are dated, but some are not. Most are signed, either with a proper signature or with a cross for those who could not write. This indicates that these were the original records written as the evidence was presented. The pages are not numbered, although for many of them the sentences run across two or more pages, so the order of the evidence is largely preserved. However, a number of the pages are dated out of sequence (the order in which they are filed), so it is not possible unequivocally, to determine the exact order in which the evidence was given. Some of the witnesses were summonsed to appear after Mr Duke's deposition had been made and they had been identified, so inevitably their evidence is out of sequence. Mr Duke's four charges seem to have been examined in the order in which they were presented to the Home Secretary, i.e. the case of George Wheeler, followed by a boy and two girls being excessively and cruelly punished, and finally the allegation of an old woman being locked up for twenty-four hours on bread and water and without straw to sleep on. Since there is a little ambiguity in the order of witness statements, and in the interests of dramatic licence, they will be presented here with the most serious case, that of George Wheeler, last.

Edward Duke had charged that an old lady, Mary King, had been locked up by the master in the refractory ward, called 'the blind house' by the paupers and others, for twenty-four hours on bread and water. Mr Duke now made a deposition in support of that charge. He had gone to the house of Thomas Stokes, Mary King's son-in-law, and there met her daughter and granddaughter. They confirmed to him that Mary King had been locked up in the blind house by the master for twenty-four hours, without a bed or any straw, and was obliged to sleep on the flint floor. This had happened, he said, four years ago.

Swayne questioned Duke about his refusal to give Mr Parker a list of witnesses. Duke said it was for private reasons; there had been a 'misunderstanding' between them. On Mrs King, he said he had known her for forty years, he knew her to be angry and violent, and knew that she had been before the board. He did not recollect that she had 'ever bitten and torn flesh out of other inmates arms'. He could not remember where he had heard rumours of Mary King's treatment.

Elizabeth Stokes, Mary King's daughter, was called. She said that her mother told her that the master had put her in the blind house, flinging her on the floor. He brought her bread and water and she threw it at him; she added, 'My mother is a little hasty sometimes'. However, she had also told her that she always had plenty to eat. Mrs Stokes did not go to Mr Duke to complain, 'I don't know but what Mr Duke is too ready to eavesdrop the grievances of the poor'. Mr Duke now questioned her. Her mother had only told her she was brought bread and water; she had not mentioned that she had no straw to sleep on.

Mrs Stokes' nineteen-year-old daughter, Ann King, was called next. Her father was dead* and she had been in the workhouse along with her grandmother at the time of the incident. She was able to explain the circumstances leading to Mary King being locked up. Some of the workhouse children, along with herself, had been taken 'up on the hill'. One of the children, the son of Fanny Thomas, had dirtied his frock. He was in the care of another pauper, Sarah Horner, who was 'beating' the child. Mary King took exception to the punishment, one thing led to another, and she ended up being confined for twenty-four hours. She had told her granddaughter that she had only bread and water and had to sleep on the flints of the floor. Ann King admitted that her grandmother was 'troublesome at times' and used to swear.

Mary King herself was called next, and confirmed some of what had already been said. She was seventy-nine years old and had been in the workhouse for seven years. She conceded that she had got into trouble over Fanny Thomas's child, but:

> I were only put in the hole—that was all—the master gave me the same as the rest—he did not hurt me—he was very good to me.

She had said that if the child were hers, she would put it on her back and travel the country rather than it should be hurt. When she came out of the hole, she said 'the child was put to me'. She said that she and the master went down the yard 'a-quarrelling' and she had called him 'a long legged son of a whore', but claimed that they were good friends afterwards; 'I won't have a word to say against my master'. And rather than bread and water, she had had bread, cheese, and tea when

---

* He was probably George Macklin, and Ann's surname suggests that she was born out of wedlock.

she was in the hole, and slept on straw albeit it was wet. She complained about it to the master the next day, although:

> I have been in here seven years and they never did me any hurt. I never heard that the Governor did any hurt to anyone in the house ... He did not keep me on bread and water as he does some of them. He kept me well but I should have liked to have had a drop of something to drink.

And regarding her family:

> I don't a-seed my daughter. My daughter and granddaughter are just above me—they won't own me. That 'ere woman my daughter is a bad one and if I had my way[?] I'd give her this stick. I did truckle the cups out after the Governors heels. I won't say I did not wet the straw—I had no other use for the cups except I used them as Mrs London* once did—Mrs London once made water in one and threw it out of the window. You'd have had no fun if I had not been here—no one shall speak about my master.

No doubt there were some wry smiles at Mrs King's forthright manner of speaking.

Pauline Conduit now deposed that she was washing Fanny Thomas's child, which was crying, when Granny King started abusing her. After arguing with the master, she was locked up. Mary Sopp gave evidence that she had brought two armfuls of straw which appeared to be dry. She added that she was in the workhouse for five years, the master was very kind indeed, and she had heard no complaints from other inmates. She confirmed that she took plenty of straw to the blind house and that it was dry; she threw it towards the back of the room, so if Mary King had thrown a cup of water at the master, it should not have wetted the straw. The last witness in respect of Mary King was Richard Wilson, who confirmed that Mary King had been brought before the board more than once for

---

* This may have been Mary Ann London.

misconduct, 'On one occasion she was brought in for tearing pieces of flesh out of another woman's arm'.

The reality of the situation must have been clear to everyone present after these witnesses had been examined. Mary King had a reputation for being refractory, violent, and abusive, and had come to the notice of the board more than once for bad behaviour. She, herself, admitted to verbally abusing the master of the workhouse, using for those days, barely printable language, and she had spent twenty-four  hours in the 'blind room' sleeping not on the flint floor, but on straw. However, the lady herself effectively admitted that she deserved it, and she was not fed on bread and water which the master did for some miscreants. She said that she and the master got on well, and would hear nothing against him. And if the straw was wet, it is eminently possible that she inadvertently wet it herself when she threw the cup at him. All the master could be accused of in the case of Mary King, was having done his duty with a lot more sympathy and consideration than Mrs King might have deserved.

At the time, accusations of brutality and ill-treatment towards children were treated more seriously than the opening chapters of *Oliver Twist* might have us believe. Mr Duke had charged that the master beat a boy and two girls on different occasions. The less serious of the two accusations, since it appeared not to have resulted in injury, will be considered first.

As before, the evidence commenced with a deposition from Mr Duke. Elizabeth Stokes, Mary King's daughter, had told him that the wife of 'James Coles' would give him information about the master having beaten two girls with a rope. Mrs Coles had told him that she and her daughter were working in the workhouse washroom, and they saw the master in an adjacent room or building (unclear from the wording) beating two girls named Sainsbury and Holmes with a rope. After the master had gone, they examined the shoulders and arms of the girls and found that they were marked with weals from the rope.

There was now a confusion of names relating to the two primary witnesses, the wife and daughter of James Coles. The wife was identified in Parker's evidence as Elizabeth *Cool*, wife of *William Cool* of Woodford. Also examined was the daughter, Jane Cool, aged twelve. The 1841 census for Woodford, records the family of William and Elizabeth *Coole*, and their daughter Jane, aged nine, so evidently it was Elizabeth Cool/Coole, the wife of William Cool/Coole, that Mr Duke had spoken to, having remembered the name of her husband and her surname incorrectly.

Elizabeth Cool had been in the workhouse for a few months from February 1843. She was working in the washhouse with Fanny Sainsbury when she heard a child cry. She saw nothing, but a child was brought to the washhouse with red marks across its shoulders. That was all she could say about it. She saw no rope. She said that the 'governor', whom she called master, behaved very well to her children. Responding to questions from Mr Swayne, she said that Mr Duke had come to her at her house. He asked her about Mary King, George Wheeler, and Moses Spreadbury (he was a key witness in the case of George Wheeler). She told him that she had heard that Spreadbury was disturbed in his mind, and she had heard the story about Wheeler being ill-used. Her daughter Jane told Mr Duke that she had seen the master beat Sarah Sainsbury. Elizabeth denied telling Mr Duke that she saw the master beating two girls with a rope, and never heard anyone tell him so in her house. She denied telling Mr Duke that she examined the girls' bruises afterwards, and denied she told him they were covered with weals, and she said that her daughter Jane was in the schoolhouse, not with her.

Her daughter Jane was examined next. She said she saw the master beat Ann Holmes and Sarah Sainsbury, although she said subsequently that she only saw Sarah Sainsbury beaten.

*Fig 1.* Edward Duke, circa 1846, from his book *Druidical Temples of the County of Wilts.*

*Fig 2.* Watercolour of Lake House painted by John Buckler in 1805, the year Edward Duke inherited the house. The picture is stated to be a 'south view', although by comparison with other contemporary illustrations and modern photographs, the house, as shown, is facing south west, and the view is from the west. Lake House is a substantial pile, and this can be gauged from the height of the front door.

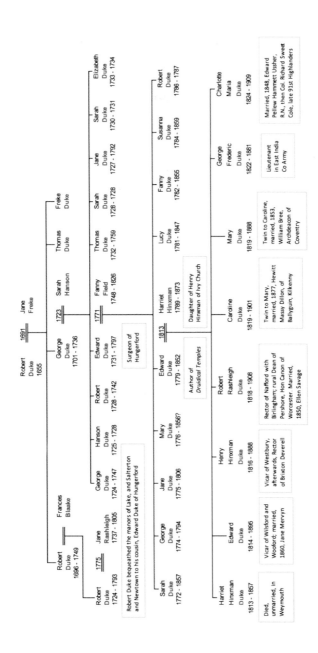

*Fig 3.* Edward Duke's family tree, from his great-grandparents to his children.

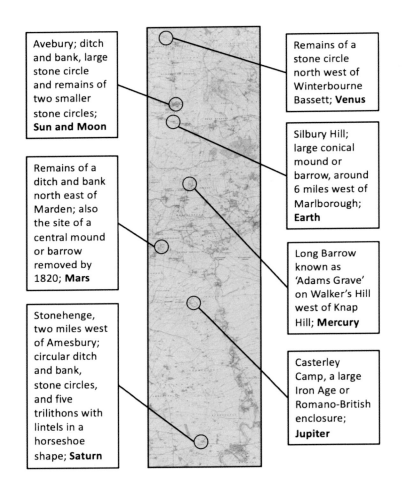

Avebury; ditch and bank, large stone circle and remains of two smaller stone circles; **Sun and Moon**

Remains of a stone circle north west of Winterbourne Bassett; **Venus**

Silbury Hill; large conical mound or barrow, around 6 miles west of Marlborough; **Earth**

Remains of a ditch and bank north east of Marden; also the site of a central mound or barrow removed by 1820; **Mars**

Long Barrow known as 'Adams Grave' on Walker's Hill west of Knap Hill; **Mercury**

Stonehenge, two miles west of Amesbury; circular ditch and bank, stone circles, and five trilithons with lintels in a horseshoe shape; **Saturn**

Casterley Camp, a large Iron Age or Romano-British enclosure; **Jupiter**

*Fig 4.* Edward Duke's 'Planetarium'; a section of the 1890s 6 inch Ordnance Survey, from Winterbourne Bassett in the north, to Amesbury in the south, a distance of about 20 miles.

| Map extracts to same scale except magnified where indicated | Description and designated 'planet' | Distance from Silbury Hill | Average distance of 'planet' from Earth normalised to Saturn = 16 in arbitrary units |
|---|---|---|---|
| x1 | Stone circle (within the rectangular field) near Winterbourne Bassett; **Venus** | 4 miles north | 1.7 |
| x1 | Avebury; **Sun and Moon** | 1 mile north | Sun 1.7<br><br>Moon 0.004 |
| x2 | Silbury Hill; **Earth** | — | — |
| x2 | Long Barrow on Walker's Hill; **Mercury** | 3 miles south | 1.7 |
| x1 | Ditch and bank near Marden; **Mars** | 6 miles south | 2.5 |
| x1 | Casterley Camp; **Jupiter** | 9 miles south | 8.8 |
| x2 | Stonehenge; **Saturn** | 16 miles south | 16.0 |

*Fig 5.* Detail of the planetarium elements: 3rd column, distances from Duke's book—accurate to about 10% from the Ordnance Survey; 4th column, average *relative* distances of the planets from Earth (*not* given in Duke's book) and normalized to the actual distance of Saturn for comparison with the planetarium. The *average* distances of Mercury and Venus from Earth are the same as Earth's distance from the Sun.

*Fig 6.* Photograph of the Amesbury Union Workhouse, early twentieth century, looking north west. Amesbury is in the background. A gloomy and foreboding aspect, evidently taken in winter.

*Fig 7. (opposite page)* Layout of the Amesbury Union Workhouse from the 1890s 25 inch Ordnance Survey. Situated less than half a mile south east of the town centre, the building was very close to the river, although elevated more than 20 feet above it. Nevertheless, the area must have been cold and damp except in summer months, made worse at times of flooding.

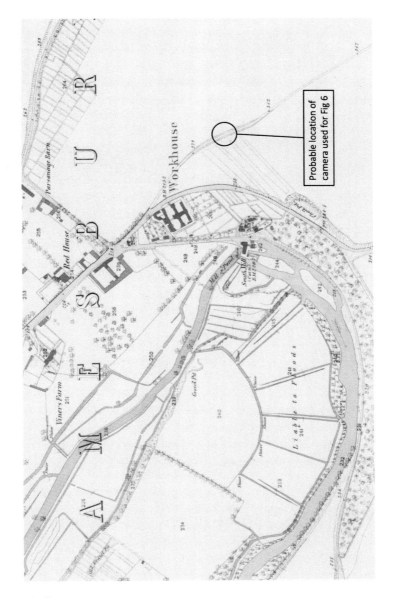

Probable location of
camera used for Fig 6

*Fig 7*

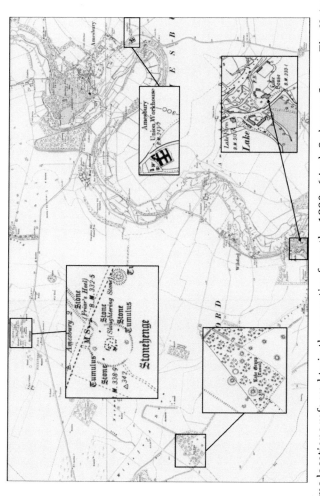

*Fig 8.* Some locations referred to in the narrative from the 1890s 6 inch Ordnance Survey. The Union Workhouse, right; Lake and Lake house (arrowed) at the bottom; the Prophet Barrows—marked *'The Lake Group'*—left; and Stonehenge at the top. The distance from Lake House to Stonehenge is around two miles.

Sarah had been combing another girl's hair. She did not know what was used for the beating. She had never seen the master with a rope, and she only ever saw Sarah Sainsbury beaten.

The two little girls, Sarah Sainsbury and Ann Holmes were now examined. Sarah was ten years old. She had been crawling about the schoolroom and said that the master gave her a smack on the ear, she cried, and her mother came to her. That was the only time she was ever beaten. Ann Holmes, also ten years old, was 'beaten' at the same time but did not cry. The master had used his hand, it was not a hard slap and 'did not hurt much'. She told her mother the master had given her a slap on the ear. Her mother then took her outside to look at her in the light, but said that there were no bruises. Sarah added:

> I was combing Holmes hair. I had got the comb from the comb
> bag and was scrambling away when the Governor came in.

She said that her mother had given her a harder slap than that she had received from the master. Ann Holmes confirmed the details. However, she said the master never beat her; she did not call a slap with a flat hand a beating. The master never beat her with a rope, and she never saw him beat any girl with a rope.

Eliza Allen was called next. Sarah Sainsbury had said that Allen was present when the so-called beating took place. Eliza Allen was sixteen years old. She only saw the master strike Ann Holmes for crawling under tables. She then said:

> Ann Holmes was under the table. I did not see Sainsbury there
> [under the table]. I know Fanny Sainsbury was there [in the
> room] because [she] came across from the Laundry and said if
> it was her child she would kick up a devil of a row. She did not
> kick up a row because the child was not hit.

She finished by saying:

> This had escaped my recollection, but it was recalled ... by Mr
> Duke coming and kicking up such a row in the house.

The evidence from these witnesses did conflict in some details—were the two girls 'beaten' together or separately? But whether or not there were 'red marks' on one of the girls, both said that rather than a beating with a rope, they had just received a cuff on the ear from the master for crawling around on the floor, and possibly for taking a comb; one of them said that her mother had slapped her harder.

In the context of the time, this was hardly child cruelty, and certainly the charge of beating with a rope hard enough to leave weals seemed to be untrue. The girls themselves denied it, and all witnesses said that they had never seen the master with a rope. Furthermore, there is some evidence from the confusion of names and the memory of who saw what and who said what to whom, to suggest that Mr Duke was more than a little muddled in his initial evidence since so much of it was denied by the witnesses.

The far more serious charge, that of physical injury to a boy from beating with a rope was detailed, as before, by Mr Duke. He said that he went to see the son of a Mrs Player of Great Durnford. He had heard rumours that the boy had received a chastisement in the workhouse resulting in a wound. Mrs Player, he said, had visited her son the following day, quite casually, to see that he had a great gash on his cheek, deep enough to lay her finger in. It took some weeks to heal. She said that the master told her that the boy had fallen out of bed and cut his cheek on the iron bedstead. Duke said that the initial rumour may have originated with Mrs London. She had been the boy's bedmaker, and told Mr Duke that the account was true and that the boy's back was covered in bruises and weals. He then spoke to another boy, John Conduit, also in the workhouse, who was present when this beating took place. He said that they had been making a noise in their bedroom over that of the old men in the room beneath; the master then came in and beat all the boys, Player more than the others.

Mr Swayne cross-examined Duke. He asked him whether he knew the boy, and where he first heard the rumour. Duke said that he was sure the mother had told him the wound was deep enough to lay her finger in. He had seen a rope, looped, with a knot in the middle, in the master's office. He was asked specific details about the rope, and how thick it was and whether the ends were tied. Duke responded that a mariner friend of his had told him that just such a rope was used at sea for punishing sailors. Duke was asked whether the rope was the size of a bell-rope. He had tried to get the master's rope from him but he refused. He had not asked the board to enquire about the use of the rope. He thought that the master's rope was larger than a piece of rope cut from the workhouse bell-rope for the purposes of the enquiry. He had not given the boy any money (for telling him what had happened). He said that the boy told him that he thought the blow that cut his cheek was not aimed at him but another boy.

Mrs Player's son was now examined. His name was actually James Coles and he was fourteen years old. His father had died when he was quite small, and his mother remarried in 1833; her name was given in the marriage register as 'Cole'. This must have been the source of Mr Duke's confusion between James/William and *Coles, Cole, Cool*, and *Coole*. James Coles had been in the workhouse on at least three occasions. Responding to questions by Mr Duke he said:

> I remember that I was beat very much in the Workhouse by the Governor ... We had been at play in our bedroom over the old men's room. The Governor came up with a rope's end in his hand and beat us with it ... He beat me ... I was out of bed at play—the blows fell about my back ... He made marks about my back—my skin was not broken but the blood was ready to come out.

It would appear then, that his cheek had not been cut, but his story did start to vary as the examination proceeded. He was examined by Mr Swayne. The boy said that he thought he

117

deserved the flogging; the master did not beat him often and when he did it was not without 'reasonable and probable cause'. The rope used was about double the size of a waggon line or the bell-rope. He said the master came on them so quickly they could not get back into bed. After some minor points about what he did and didn't say to Mr Duke, he mentioned John Williams. Williams was a pauper schoolmaster, now dead, who used to sleep in the same room as the boys. He used a rope on the boys during the day, and beat him (Coles) about the face once in the bedroom, cutting him below the eye. It did not bleed much, and it was not long enough to put his finger in. John Conduit was in the room at the time. Coles never told the master about it. Jane Conduit and Mrs London saw the cut the next morning. In response to a question from Mr Swayne, he said:

> I told Mr Duke the rope slipped almost out of the Governor's hand and took me in the same place and made it bad again. I told him I was in bed at the time. I can't mind how long it was the Governor beat me after Williams beat me. I was out of bed when the Governor struck me.

His interlocutors sensed that he was shifting his story, and possibly in response to a question from the chaplain he said:

> I do not know the nature of an oath. I go to Sunday School. The Catechism is said there not very often … I did not learn it … I have heard the good will go to Heaven and the wicked will go to Hell. If I tell an untruth it will be a lie.

Mr Swayne took up the questioning again. Coles said: 'I cannot say no more'. He couldn't remember telling Ruth Batchellor about the incident,[*] he couldn't remember whether John and Richard Conduit were present when he was talking to her, and

---

[*] A conversation with Ruth Batchellor was referred to by several other witnesses later on. This evidence from Coles may have been filed out of order.

he couldn't remember whether he said that Williams had cut a piece out of his face, however:

> He [Williams] did cut the piece out of my cheek and bring the blood up. John Williams did not cut my face more than once. I don't know what he bothered me for.

He said he did not know that Williams and Spreadbury were not good friends. Then he said: 'He [Williams] beat me because I wouldn't make a noise over Spreadbury's head. He beat a good many of them'. But literally his next statement was: 'Williams beat us not to make a noise. We were making a noise when Williams beat us'. He now said that he was fully dressed in the bedroom when Williams cut him about the eye, and he continued to claim that the master came into the room (on a different occasion) and struck him and several other boys. He never told anyone he had fallen out of bed. He heard the master tell his mother he had, but when he went home, he told her it was not true. He claimed that when the master hit him, about a month after Williams, he hit him in the same place and it bled. And now he said he did not know why he told Mr Swayne he had been in bed; he didn't know why he told Mr Duke the blow was intended for another boy. Questioned by Mr Duke, he said he should not know the rope again, although he had told Rev Mr Duke he should know it.

James Coles' mother, Mary Ann Player, was now examined. She had been in the workhouse, along with her husband and children, but was not there at same time as James Coles. She related how the master had explained James's cut face being caused by him falling out of bed. She said she could have 'laid her finger in [the cut]'. Questioned by Mr Swayne, she said that John Williams had told her that the master had beaten James whilst he was in bed. The boy had told her the same, and he did not say that anyone other than the master had struck him. She said the wound was as wide as her finger—she did not recall telling Mr Duke that it was deep enough to lay her finger in. She, herself, was treated well in the workhouse.

Having said that she had never considered asking Duke to complain on her behalf, she said that the boy told her that Williams had beaten him, although he never told her that it was Williams who had cut his face. It all took place four years ago, and she had mentioned it to a few people although not the guardian of the parish. She had never heard other reports of ill-usage.

John Conduit was now examined. He was also fourteen years old, and remembered that Coles received a cut face, but it was from the 'master', John Williams, using a rope. He clarified that they called the master 'governor' and the schoolmaster 'master'.* John Conduit said that Coles was beaten by Williams because he would not get out of bed and make a noise to annoy Moses Spreadbury, who was in the room below. Conduit said that Coles was in bed when he was beaten, and he also received six blows across the back, and he said that the master did not come in that night. Spreadbury had sworn at the boys the next day for making a noise. John Conduit said that his mother (Jane Conduit?) dressed the wound the next day. He said that he never knew the master to beat the boys without the knowledge of the board, or to come to their bedroom to beat the boys, or to use a rope to beat them. He finished his evidence by saying that his mother was angry with him for talking to Mr Duke about the incident.

Mary Ann London, the bedmaker, was now questioned by Mr Duke. She said that Coles told her it was the master who beat him, although she could not be sure he did not say 'master', i.e. the schoolmaster. Mr Swayne took over the questioning and she told him that James May, another boy, had just told

---

* As noted previously, Mr Ralfs was sometimes referred to as the *Master*, sometimes the *Governor*, by different people, and this was to lead to some confusion. Similarly, Mrs Ralfs was referred to variously as the *Mistress*, the *Matron*, and sometimes just the *Mrs*.

her that Coles was now saying that it was Williams who beat him: 'I said if he did he must be a bad boy to say the master had a-done it'. She also denied saying that May or anyone else had been bribed to say 'a false truth'. She said that Coles had told her that he was punished because the boys were throwing their bedclothes at each other and making a noise, not because they were not making a noise. She didn't think that Williams slept in the boys' dormitory.

James May was now examined. He was sixteen and had been in the workhouse at the time of Coles' beating. He said Coles was wounded near the eye by Williams hitting him with a rope. It was not done by the master, although:

> I have known the Governor give the boys a stroke or two when we have got flinging the clothes about.

He said he saw John Williams do it. He had had no conversation with Mrs Player or Mrs London about the case, other than when Mrs London asked him whether it was Williams or the master who had hurt Coles. He said Coles told him it was Williams. Since he had left the workhouse, he had often been back to see Mr and Mrs Ralfs who had been kind to him. Questioned by Mr Duke, he said the master had given the boys a stroke or two with a slipper in the bedroom. Never a rope. He did use a rope downstairs which he kept in his office.

The next witness was called to establish what sort of rope was used in the navy for disciplining sailors. This was presumably because Duke had implied that since Ralfs had been a navy man, that would explain his preference for using a rope on the boys. Thomas Davis had spent nearly twenty years at sea. He was dismissive of the length of bell-rope he was shown (but this was not the rope that had been used by the master, so the exercise seemed to be somewhat futile). He said that the rope used on sailors was always bound at the end to stop it unravelling; it was always far thicker than the rope he had been shown, and was stiffened with tar.

The last two witnesses were boys who were also present in the dormitory when Coles was beaten. Richard Conduit, eleven years old, said that John Williams came round at daybreak and told Coles to get out of bed to tease Spreadbury. He refused, and was beaten while still in bed, cutting his cheek. He said that he had heard Coles telling another pauper, Ruth Batchellor, that it was Williams who had struck him in the face. William Macklin, twelve years old, confirmed the story, as well as the conversation with Ruth Batchellor, saying that he too saw Williams do it.

The evidence from James Coles was highly unsatisfactory, since he shifted his story several times. In his summary of the evidence, Parker commented on Coles:

> This boy prevaricated whilst under examination and when asked respecting the blow given by Williams he reluctantly answered. His statement is not consistent in some respects and his manner of giving evidence was restrained and very different from that of the other boys.

Nevertheless, the evidence of four other boys present was unequivocal: James Coles was hit in the face by Williams using a length of rope while he [Coles] was still in bed, and it had cut his cheek. The third of Mr Duke's charges, it seems, was entirely false.

Examination of the most serious charge, the enquiry into which caused this book to be written, commenced as before, with a deposition from Edward Duke. Violent cruelty, probably leading to premature death, was perpetrated by the workhouse master against George Wheeler, a fifteen-year-old crippled, orphan pauper.[*] This had taken place four years earlier.

George Wheeler, whose family were from the parish of Figheldean, had had a short and unhappy life. In May 1838 when

---

[*] See Appendix 4 for evidence of George Wheeler's age and details of his family.

George was about thirteen, his mother, Sarah, had died of what was called 'decline', a catchall description for some wasting disease. His father, David, died a year later of consumption. There were five children in the family, and it is a measure of their general state of health, that after George had died only his brother Charles, and a younger sister Mary, were still alive. George was born with a condition where his hamstring tendons were abnormally contracted, making it impossible to stand or walk. He also suffered from consumption, and to compound the misery of his final days, he was racked with vomiting and diarrhoea. His brother Charles, around seven years his junior, was also an inmate of the workhouse. George had three aunts, Mary Clift, Elizabeth Rumbold, and Susannah Thomas. Mary who lived in Figheldean, and Elizabeth, living in Durrington, were his father's sisters; Susannah, who lived in Allington, was sister to his mother.

Mr Duke now presented his charges. He had not known George Wheeler, but had heard rumours of his ill-treatment a few weeks previously. He went to see James Fry, a pauper from the workhouse, who was at that time in the Salisbury Infirmary. Fry made a statement concerning an assault by the workhouse master on George Wheeler. After that he interviewed, on the second attempt, a blind pauper in the workhouse, Moses Spreadbury, whom he admitted was in a 'very perturbed state of mind'. Spreadbury had said that he slept in the same room (the infirmary) as Wheeler, although he was not there when the assault took place. He was walking across the court and heard the cry of 'Murder!' He went into the infirmary where Wheeler was crying. Fry told him that the master 'had used Wheeler very ill'. He was bleeding from the head and blood was coming out of his ears. Spreadbury said that the workhouse guardian representing Durrington (probably Spreadbury's home parish) had asked him why he had not previously reported it, and he said he did not dare to; the master had threatened to 'confine' him if he spoke about it.

Mr Duke interviewed another pauper, John Pothecary, who saw Wheeler about half an hour after the assault had occurred, and he affirmed that there was blood on his head. Duke added that he had received information from no-one else, 'more than second-hand rumours, and those I did not attend to.'

Duke was now cross-examined by Mr Swayne, and said that he believed he had heard the rumour initially from Mrs London, a washerwoman he had known from when she was in the workhouse, and to whom he gave 'trifles'. He had met her in the street, and she told him of the death of 'the boy Wheeler', but begged he wouldn't use her name in case she had to go back in the workhouse where she would 'suffer for it'. She had told him that Fry could give him more information. He had also heard gossip from one Charlotte Clark in the gaol where he was visiting magistrate; she was there for absconding from the workhouse. He then recalled that he had heard talk about Wheeler two or three years ago, but his 'misplaced confidence in the Master lulled (him) to sleep'. In response to questions from Mr Swayne, he said that he had brought some charges against the master two years ago, but had 'broken off' the enquiry having no proof. Then:

> I am dissatisfied with this mode of examination now—I never heard such a cross-examination as this at [Quarter] Sessions.

Mr Duke had made this point several times in his letters to the PLC following the 1842 enquiry. It may be that in his capacity as a law officer bringing a charge, Mr Duke did not regard himself as a prosecution witness, and therefore should not be cross-examined. He was asked why he suspected the master of 'improperly chastising the paupers', and claimed it was when he saw a rope hanging up in the master's office and was told it was used for beating the boys.

Moses Spreadbury, one of his informants was, he was told, 'disturbed in his mind', although Duke declared: 'I never found him disturbed before that time' (presumably the time when he first tried to interview him). Furthermore:

> He [Spreadbury] is an old man and helpless and only lately he has been confined to his bed. I fancy there is nothing against his character—his character is very good. I have never heard any complaint against him.

And on his other informant, Fry:

> I heard at this Board a few weeks since that Fry was in the Salisbury infirmary ... I went to him then because I knew he would be free from any fear to disclose the truth. I have found that the paupers have been afraid to make complaints—I have been told so by them. I cannot recollect by whom but I have heard of it repeatedly out of this House.

Fry was now examined. James Fry was thirty-four years old; he was born in the parish of Idmiston and had been in the workhouse five years. He stated that his eyesight had been defective 'this twelvemonth'. He was in the sick ward, and George Wheeler had been transferred there around three months before he had died. He said Wheeler was looked after by Elizabeth Pinkney, as well as by Charles Truckle and Robert Kilford. One morning the master had come in and asked the boy why he was not up. He said he was not able to get up because he could not. The master insisted several times on his getting up, but the boy said he could not without a pillow to sit on. The master took him by one leg and one arm and threw him down on the brick floor, then picked him up and threw him on the bed. The boy cried out very much when his head struck the flint wall and was cut open. After the master left, Fry managed to get him into bed and asked if he was hurt. He said he thought he heard something 'pop' inside. There was blood on the pillow but none on the wall; he was never well after that, and died five weeks later.

Fry said that the doctor, at his request, had put a 'plaister'*
on the wound, which was at the back of the boy's head. The
wound was around half an inch long and sharp as if cut by a
knife. Elizabeth Pinkney washed and dressed the wound, and
used scissors to cut the hair off around it. Fry said that the
wound healed up in two weeks, although the boy was in very
bad health afterwards, always complaining of his bowels:

> As soon as he did take anything, it was through him either
> upwards or downwards. He was in that state till he died, night
> and day at times.

He added that also in the ward at the time were Abraham
Joules, Joseph Ellis and William Witt—the last two now being
dead. He was now examined by Mr Swayne. Wheeler was, he
said, a cripple who had no use of his limbs (he meant his legs).
Fry would lift him in and out of bed and dress him sometimes.
Elizabeth Pinkney, who also looked after him, was not there
during the assault, and had now gone to a foreign country.
He seemed to be uncertain whether Elizabeth Pinkney or the
doctor had brought the plaister; she certainly had washed the
boy's head. Dr Pyle, the workhouse medical officer, arrived
two or three hours after the assault, and saw Wheeler several
times a week. Fry said he remembered hearing Wheeler tell
the doctor how the wound happened. He said the boy's friends
and also one of the other inmates, Jane Conduit, came to see
him.

Fry said that Abraham Joules was bedridden (as he still
was); his bed was at the foot of Wheeler's bed. After the incident
several people came into the ward—Elizabeth Pinkney, Charles
Kilford, John Pothecary, who saw some blood, and Moses
Spreadbury. Fry declared that he had never mentioned the

---

* A Plaister was 'a solid medicinal or emollient substance spread on a
bandage or dressing and applied to the skin, often becoming adhesive at
body temperature', *Oxford English Dictionary*.

incident to the guardians when they walked around the house, that the master had threatened to punish him if he talked, and that Dr Pyle told him he ought to be 'kicked out of the yard gates' for accusing the master. Fry said that he told the boy's friends; he said they were women (and were probably George Wheeler's aunts), but he did not tell Mr Duke; he added:

> Mr. Duke used to ask us whether we had complaints to make. I was not afraid to tell Mr. Duke anything. I did not tell him [about Wheeler] because I thought it was not my business as the boy's friends did not report it.

However, he said next: 'I have spoken of this very often and a great deal. It was talked of for a very long while'. Then, 'I should have told if the boy's friends had put forward for it.' He said he thought it was an accident; that the master had not intended to hurt the boy. He denied saying that blood had gushed from the boy's ears. Fry said that the master had not ill-used him, apart from the threat not to tell on him, but he had seen him ill-use Charles Kilford who, he alleged, said to the master 'are you going to use me the same as the other cripple boy?', at which point the master let him go.

James Fry's evidence was critical to Mr Duke's case. He was the witness who claimed that he had actually seen the assault on George Wheeler, and had provided key elements of detail which could be checked with other witnesses.

Moses Spreadbury now made his deposition. He was seventy-seven years old, and had been in the workhouse for seven years, with the last year spent in the sick ward. He was 'stone' blind, and had been so before he entered the workhouse. He said that Wheeler was 'sobbing and crying' on 12 March 1840:

> I said "what be thee'st at thy fun again?" and he said "sad fun." He said the governor had thrown him out of bed, and he said "I found something pop in my inside and I shall die. I shall not live six weeks longer, Moses, and I wish you to publish it." I said "I shan't" and he said "if you don't I am certain sure I shall

come again". I suppose he meant his ghost would visit me. I did not publish it until I was terrified like—I thought I ought to do it. I have not seen the ghost, but I have heard it, it laughed at me just in the same way it did when it was alive.

He said that he was in the doorway when he heard the boy cry out 'Murder!', but nobody rushed into the room; he said that there were three people present but did not clarify who those thee were. He said he heard Wheeler tell Elizabeth Pinkney that he would not live six weeks. He claimed to have been present when Wheeler died. Spreadbury asked Wheeler if he thought his imminent death was the master's doing. Wheeler had said 'yes'. Spreadbury said he did not know whether there was any blood on the bed after the assault: 'I never told anybody that I had felt the blood'. At what he said next, Mr Parker might have wondered whether Spreadbury was entirely sane:

> The ghost came to me and followed me for thirteen months—there were three voices, one a very rough one, another like the boy, and the other like a woman's. They kept on laughing at me—they kept on singing the service to me—they sang "My soul doth magnify the Lord". At Christmas they sang Christmas carols "God bless you merry gentlemen". Sometimes they prayed to me at midnight. I have not heard them for six weeks. I told Mr Duke about this last Thursday night.

Following a question from Mr Duke, Spreadbury said:

> The boy told me to tell of this ... ten minutes before he died ... I did not dare to do so ... The Master called us in on the Monday as the boy was buried on Sunday and he said "you have been putting about that I killed the boy" and I said "I never published it but the boy begged me to publish." He then said "Oh Moses, Oh Moses, I wish you had died as the boy died" and I said "I wish I had, Sir" The Governor threatened to lock me up if I spoke of it. He threatened to put me on the back of the fire and put his hand into my face and threatened to knock my front teeth down my throat. I said "I shall make proclamation of it to Mr. Duke" and he said "don't tell me of Mr. Duke—there

is nobody that has anything to do here but me—my house is my castle."

He answered a question from Mr Swayne:

> In 1839 Mr Duke used to come to see me two or three times a week. It was in the year 1840 the boy died ... [Duke] used to ask us if we had any complaint ... I never told Mr Duke—I did not dare. I did not promise the boy I would publish it. I said to him "George, I can't tell what to say about that." Mr Duke ... said if there were any complaints he would alter it ... I never said I saw blood or that there was blood ... Mr. Duke was always ready to hear complaints. I did not dare speak because I was afraid of my own life.

He went on to say that he had very little contact with the workhouse chaplain who refused him the Sacrament. And responding to further questions about Wheeler's injuries, he said that he felt the injuries, and 'felt something wet', but could not tell whether it was blood or water. He never said he 'saw' blood coming from Wheeler's eyes and ears.

James Fry was then recalled and questioned by Mr Swayne. He was present, he said, when the boy died, as was Elizabeth Pinkney, the master, his wife, and 'little before he died' Joules, Ellis and Witt. Truckle was not there when Wheeler died, neither was Spreadbury. Furthermore, 'The boy could not speak and had not been able [to] all the night before'. He did say that he had heard Wheeler telling Charles Truckle 'a good many times' that the master threw him out of bed.

Fry and Spreadbury were Mr Duke's authority for his charge against the master. Their version of events disagreed as to who was present and who was not when George Wheeler died, but then it had all taken place four years ago. Quite what Mr Parker made of Spreadbury and his ghosts he did not reveal.

Now, the only other living eyewitness to the incident was called. Abraham Joules, or Joles, had no idea of his age, although the census marked him as sixty in 1841. He had been in the workhouse for four years; always in the sick ward. Regarding George Wheeler and the alleged assault:

> I recollect ... the governor telling George Wheeler to get out of bed and he would not and the governor then drawed him out of bed ... After the governor pulled him out the governor put him in again ... Some of them said there was blood at his head but I did not see it. I was pretty near asleep but was awaked by the bustle ... I tell you sir, the governor put him down on the floor ... His body touched the floor, the boy cried out but I can't tell what he said. Nobody came in when he made a noise.

He said that Isaac Kite, now dead, was in the ward at the time; Ellis was there also. Then,

> Nobody came to dress the boy's head. Someone said there was blood. I don't know whether anyone washed the blood away. There was no blood to signify. I did not see the doctor come. I did not see any plaister used. If anyone had put plaister on his head I would have seen it ... Some of them said there was nothing ... worth putting on a plaister. Nobody came with scissors and cut his hair off.

And when George Wheeler died:

> There was a main sight of people there ... Spreadbury was not in the room ... I don't think Charles Truckle was there ... I did not hear the boy speak on the morning that he died. I could see him. I can't mind whether Mrs Ralfs came into the room on the morning.

Mr Duke asked him to clarify again what had happened:

> I said the master took the boy out of bed and pulled him down on the floor—that is all. Governor did not pull him out with violence. He did not throw him on the floor with violence. When he was on the floor he put him in bed again but not with violence—he was afraid he should be hurt. He cried out but what he cried out I can't mind. I did not hear Fry ask him anything—if he did I have forgotten it ... I was wide awake when this happened, I was awaked by the bustle. The boy

never said anything to me about it—he said he was bad in his inside.

This was a very different version of what had happened from what Fry had stated. There was no violence, 'no blood to speak of', and no plaister. Joules insisted that he was wide awake, although he said initially that he was 'pretty near asleep'. Abraham Joules was Mr Duke's third witness as to what had happened, and had been questioned by him as he stated in his deposition. It seems curious, therefore, that Duke did not recognize the quite different account related by him compared with that from James Fry, and did not make further enquiries before making his most serious charge.

John Pothecary and Charles Truckle were examined next; both had been inmates of the workhouse when the incident with George Wheeler had happened. Pothecary's story matched with that of Abraham Joules. He had been in the yard and had come into the sick ward after the incident; Fry and Spreadbury were there already, and all he knew about it was what they had told him. He saw a small scratch on Wheeler's forehead, just over his nose, with a little blood. There was no swelling and he did not hear the boy cry out, saying if he had have cried out, he would have heard him. He never saw a plaister. Charles Truckle's contribution was that George Wheeler had asked him to stay with him on the morning he died, and he did so, holding his hand until the end. On Fry and Spreadbury, he said:

> I never heard Fry talk of having done kind actions and never knew him do any. I don't think Moses Spreadbury a likely man to do kind actions.

And on the master:

> The boy never made any declarations to me ... respecting his illness. He once told me that he had fallen out with Mr Ralfs. I never recollect that he ever told me that anything Mr Ralfs had done had occasioned his illness.

Charles Pyle had been the medical officer to the Amesbury Union since its inception, and was called as the next witness. He said that George Wheeler suffered from scrofula;* he had swollen glands in the neck and contractions of the knees. Pyle did not treat Wheeler for any 'contused or incised wound of the head', and had no record of having supplied him with a plaister which, he said, he would have entered in his 'pauper day book'. Wheeler also suffered from 'bilious vomiting and ... diarrhoea', which was endemic in the workhouse and surrounding area at the time. During the week of 6 April 1840, Wheeler was entered in the medical relief list as suffering from consumption, from which he died on 17 April 1840. There were 'no symptoms in the case that proceeded from a violent contusion'; he added that the consumption gave the boy a delicate constitution. Mr Pyle did not remember having been examined by the board at the time, although he did remember the incident having been brought to the board's notice.

Mr Pyle was asked about Moses Spreadbury; he had been receiving medical treatment for a long time:

> I should give him a very bad character. He is frequently making complaints. On investigation I find them without the slightest foundation.

Pyle was now examined by Mr Duke, and in response to various questions said:

> the boy had diarrhoea on him to the day of his death. If the boy had a very severe blow in the stomach ... sickness ... would occur in a very few hours. I forgot to mention the boy was suffering from a constant cough. I do not think diarrhoea would follow a blow on the head. If I had been told this boy had a severe blow on the head and that was followed by vomiting and diarrhoea, I should attribute the vomiting and diarrhoea to such a blow ... The boy was taking opium and chalk and other medicine.

---

* 'probably a form of tuberculosis', *Oxford English Dictionary.*

Following questions from Mr Swayne, he said that Wheeler had never complained to him of having been hurt. There was not the slightest appearance of any head wound when he examined the boy post mortem, and such a wound as had been claimed would not have healed up in five weeks given his delicate constitution. He admitted, however, that if the wound had been at the back of the head, he might not have seen it. Fry had never told him about the boy's wound on the head and he never saw blood on the wall or pillow.

He had heard Spreadbury and a few others abuse the master, but in general the paupers, the children particularly, spoke very highly of him, and he knew that Mr Ralfs sent food from his own table to Wheeler. He denied threatening Fry with being kicked out of the yard gates for what he said about the master. Mr Duke now had some questions for Mr Pyle; he responded:

> [Wheeler] was at that age when young people are commonly affected by consumption. Scrofulous disease of the lungs carried him off ... I recognised the symptoms of consumption about a fortnight before the boy died.

However:

> I consider death arising in a fortnight is a very rapid consumption indeed ... Cases of consumption usually terminate with diarrhoea [but] consumption alone did not carry off the boy, but a combination of diseases.

On the question of violence:

> If this boy had had such a blow as would produce vomiting and diarrhoea there would have been visible evidence of the violence ... If this boy had received a wound it would in all probability have become a permanent wound and would not have healed.

And whether Wheeler had been treated with a plaister:

> I am certain—quite confident that I should not entrust a
> nurse to bind up and plaister a wound on the first occasion
> of treating it.

He finished his evidence by making a pointed comment about
Mr Duke:

> I have frequently seen Mr. Duke for some time past and indeed
> have been attending him. He never conferred with me on this
> case. If he had been desirous of ascertaining the ... state of the
> serious trauma I am the person to apply to most undoubtedly.

Mr Pyle's evidence conflicted with that of Fry and Spreadbury,
and appeared to corroborate that of Joules, Pothecary, and
Truckle. It is curious though, that he remembered the incident
being brought before the board, but did not recall being
examined. He did appear flatly to contradict any possibility of
a plaister having been applied to the alleged wound.

Next on the stand was Mary Ann London, whom Mr Duke
claimed was the first person who told him of the affair. She was
a washerwoman, living in Salisbury, and had been an inmate
of the workhouse at the time of George Wheeler's death. She
used to wash his face and make his bed. She never saw any
blood on his bed. He used to complain to her that the back of
his head was bad and he had a pain in the chest. Questioned
by Mr Swayne, she denied that Mr Duke had ever talked to
her about George Wheeler, and never said that he was cruelly
used. She never told him that Wheeler's brother burst into
tears when he heard about it, and never told Mr Duke not
to use her name in the context of George Wheeler. She had
spoken to Mr Duke about a boy of the name Coles whose bed
she made, and who had a cut on his face. Coles had told her
that the master had done it because 'they' were making a noise
over the old men's heads. She did ask Mr Duke not to use her
name in connection with the story about Coles in case she had
to go back into the workhouse. Duke had mentioned Wheeler
to her, she knew him but had nothing to do with him (although

she had said earlier that she washed his face and made his bed). She told Duke to ask Fry about him. She knew Mr Duke in the workhouse, and now saw him in the street from time to time; occasionally he gave her money. He had tried to get relief for her from the board to help with her rent but had not succeeded. Her daughter used to be in the workhouse, and Mr Ralfs had not used either of them 'ill'. Her daughter had come to Amesbury twice since leaving the workhouse, with the sole purpose of seeing Mr and Mrs Ralfs out of her regard for them, particularly the 'mistress'.

The interview with Duke had taken place only three weeks previously, and he obviously got confused with what she had told him, and what he had learned from James Fry. It seems possible that Duke also became confused between what she told him about Coles' injuries sustained whilst in bed, and those of George Wheeler. What was also interesting, is that Mary Ann London's daughter, an ex pauper, had so much regard for the Ralfses, that she had twice made the journey from Salisbury to Amesbury to visit them.

The next witness was Charles Kilford. He was an inmate of the workhouse, a cripple, and had been there when George Wheeler was alive. He claimed that he was the first in the room 'after it was done'. He heard the master and Wheeler talking, and after the master had left the room asked George what had happened. He said the master had thrown him out of bed because he would not get up—he emphasised would not rather than could not. He said he was three yards from the door (outside) when this took place. Wheeler did not cry out 'murder', he said 'Oh dear'. Fry and Joules were in the room, Joules was in bed, and Fry was sitting on his bed. The boy was not crying. He saw no wound, there was no blood on the pillow or sheet, and no blood from his nose or ears. He remembered that there was some talk about the incident after Wheeler died, there was an examination before the board, and Fry was taken to the master's office. He thought that 'Mr Self' was one of the guardians present, and Mr Pyle was there. Fry, he said, had never mentioned anything about what had happened when he was examined.

Kilford said that he saw George Wheeler most days after this had happened, he never complained of having a bruise, and he never cried. He added that the master's conduct to the inmates was very good; he was very kind to them, although some of them were 'refractory'. He was now questioned by Mr Duke. Wheeler had been sick and 'bad in his bowels' before this happened. Kilford said he had never been ill-used by the master. He thought Spreadbury was a bad character and a liar, and denied asking the master if he was going to kill him as he did the cripple boy.

Now it was the turn of George Wheeler's brother, Charles, on the stand. He had only been eight years old when his brother died, but had seen him several times a day in the weeks beforehand. The master had told him that he could go and see George any time he liked. He never saw a bruise or wound on his brother's head, and his brother never complained about such a wound. He never saw any blood on the sheets or pillows, or about his face, nose, and ears. His brother had never told him that the master had pulled him out of bed, although his aunts had asked him about it and told him that the master had killed George. On the contrary, he said that the master behaved very well to George, and that George had spoken about it, even on the day he died; he said he was 'very much obliged to the master for his kindness'. Charles knew that the master had sent George food from his table, and he said that the master had been kind to him (Charles) and the other boys. He was with his brother on the morning that he died.

Mr Duke asked him some questions. Charles said that he did not hear the story about what happened to his brother until he went out of the workhouse, and he added in response to a particular question:

> I never saw any plaister on my brother's head ... If he had had
> a plaister on I should have noticed it. I am quite sure none of
> his hair was cut away and a plaister put there.

Charles Wheeler was only eight years old when his brother had died, and was still only twelve, yet his evidence has the ring of truth. Charles must have been the closest person to George in the workhouse, and if he had had any grievances in his final few hours and minutes, surely he would have told his brother. Instead, George had expressed his gratitude towards the master for his kindness. Mr Duke's case seemed to be unravelling.

Next on the stand was Jane Conduit, who should have been one of Mr Duke's staunchest allies. He had made a great fuss over his perception of the mismanagement of her case by the Amesbury Union when she was living in poverty in Salisbury. He had given her money from time to time. She was a widow who had been in the workhouse for six years, and three of her children were also in the house. She was around 50 years old. She remembered George Wheeler to whom she regularly took food, including food from the master's table. She was on friendly terms with him, and thought that he would have told her if he had been ill-used. He expressed his gratitude towards the master to her, 'frequently two or three times in a day'. She never saw a wound or bruise on his head, or a plaister, or any of his hair cut off. She said she was with him, along with Mrs Ralfs, a few minutes before he died; he expressed his gratitude to both of them for their kindness. She cited a particular instance when the master had directed some tea and buttered toast from his table to be taken to 'poor George Wheeler'. She never heard any report while Wheeler was still alive of him being ill-used by the master or anyone else. She said the rumour came into the house from the villages several weeks after Wheeler's death, and 'We all strongly denied it because we knew better'. After George Wheeler's death, she and Betty Pinkney laid him out and Betty washed the body. There was no appearance of any wound on the body. Mr Pyle, the surgeon, came the next day and cut the 'sinews of the legs' in order to put the body into the coffin. She added that when visiting George she 'never saw a speck of blood on him'.

She said that she never saw anything but kindness towards the paupers by the master. She, herself, had received kind treatment when she had been ill. Then:

> It is a very usual thing for the Governor to send food from his own table to everyone who is ill. I was employed five years out of six in the kitchen and I had opportunities of knowing. I have repeatedly carried things myself to the paupers, and when I have been ill, I have partaken of those good things.

And on the general perception of the master:

> The opinion of everyone in the house, as far as I have heard say, is that the governor is very kind to them. After inmates have been discharged from the house I have known many of them visit the house to see the governor and matron. The master and matron always appeared happy to see them.

Jane Conduit's evidence now related to Mr Duke and his activities in and out of the workhouse. She described an incident when the master was out, and Duke demanded the keys to the master's office from Mrs Ralfs; he searched the provision books in Jane's presence. He asked her why more beef was allowed in the pea soup when there were fewer inmates in the house. She related that two weeks ago, Mr Duke had asked her several questions about George Wheeler; she told him she knew nothing about Wheeler and referred him to the master and matron. On another occasion he came looking for Mrs Conduit in the workhouse, and finding that she had been sent for to visit her aged mother in Durnford, he followed her there. On one occasion, he accused her of having been instructed by Mrs Ralfs to ring the workhouse bell to indicate when Mr Duke had left. He threatened her with the 'utmost rigour of the law', but she insisted that it must have been one of the children who had rung the bell. She added:

> He then told me he had great enmity and hatred towards the Governor and he would do everything in his power to get him out of his place—he said he would likewise dismiss the whole Board of Governors if he could, for he had great enmity against them, but he well knew he could not.

He had also questioned her about James Coles. 'Mr Duke' now asked her some questions, and on Edward Duke's previous questions to her about Wheeler, she said:

> I did not choose to tell Mr. Duke what I have now said about George Wheeler, because I was weary of answering his questions ... Mr. Duke said he knew it was no good asking me questions for he knew I would not satisfy him.

When she had returned to the workhouse, she told the master and Mrs Ralfs about Mr Duke and his questions. She denied she was angry with Mr Duke when he interrupted her visit to her mother at Durnford, although: 'I was very much hurt that Mr. Duke interrupted my conversation with my mother'. She went on:

> Two or three Board days ago I did tell Mr. Duke that it was very wrong of him to question children and make them tell a lot of lies, and that he ought to apply for information to the master and matron if he wanted to know anything about the house.

Duke had also been talking to one of her children: 'Mr Duke had been asking questions of my boy ... afterwards [he] was impudent and I strapped him for his impudence'. She did recall, she said, Duke asking her if she remembered that he had saved her life.

The evidence from Jane Conduit was quite damaging. She should have been a sympathetic witness because of Duke's previous support for her. Instead, she confirmed the master's kindness, as well as George Wheeler's gratitude to Mr and Mrs Ralfs on and before the day he died. She admonished Mr Duke for asking the children questions with the evident intention of causing trouble, and complained about his presence when she was visiting her sick mother. Was it possible that Duke had really said to her what she had repeated in respect of his hatred of the master and board? If true, it would have been most astonishingly indiscreet, but then Mr Duke had quite a track record of indiscretion.

Edwin Farr was the next witness. He was one of the relieving officers, and had been so since the union was set up. Questioned by Mr Duke, he said that he had been told by Mary Clift, one of George Wheeler's aunts, that George Wheeler had been ill-treated by the master. He was in Figheldean handing out payments to paupers when she called on him, repeated the story, and asked him if he thought it was true. He reported it to the board. He thought that Fry and Mr Pyle were examined by the board. Mr Swayne now questioned him. He said that he reported back to 'the woman Clift' the results of the investigation. She said she was perfectly satisfied, adding that she only asked him because people were talking about it so much, and it was 'common conversation' in the village. Since that time, he had heard nothing of it until Mr Duke had made his recent charge.

Richard Wilson confirmed that the date of the board meeting to discuss Mrs Clift's allegation had been 4 May 1840, at which were present Rev Lowther, Mr Lang, Mr Puckham, and Mr Smith. Mr Ralfs, Mr Pyle, and one other, whom he thought was probably Betty Pinkney, were examined (but not James Fry?). He read out the minute that had been entered exonerating the master, and confirmed that it had been read through to the following meeting, which had been attended by Mr Duke. He confirmed that Mr Pyle was definitely present.

Mr Parker now called two of the guardians present at the meeting, Francis Lang (the younger) and Stephen Smith. Lang represented Bulford parish, and remembered the investigation; he also remembered that Mr Pyle was examined, as was the woman who had been nursing Wheeler, Betty Pinkney. He remembered seeing George Wheeler many times, and also that the boy had never made any complaint to him about the master's treatment of him. Mr Smith confirmed all that Lang had said. He remembered that Ralfs, Mr Pyle, and a woman were examined. He also visited George Wheeler, who never made any complaints to him. He added: 'From the opportunities I have had of judging, I think the master behaves very kindly indeed to the pauper inmates.'

The person who brought the guardians' attention to the initial rumour about George Wheeler having been assaulted was now called, she was one of George Wheeler's aunts, Mary Clift. Mary Clift, accompanied by her sister, Elizabeth Rumbold, had visited George Wheeler twice when he was ill in the workhouse. On the first occasion, they came because the master had sent for them; the second visit was made because Mr Simpkins, the guardian representing the parish of Figheldean, had told them that George was very ill and was asking for them. On the second occasion, the master had been present; when he left for a few minutes, George had said to them:

> "Aunts I have been used very ill" I said "why George, how was that"—he answered "He ordered me to get up and I was not able to get up. He then said he would throw me out if I did not get up". He said "[I] was not able to get out and he threw me out on the floor." He did not say "the Governor" but he said "he". I supposed he meant the Governor. That was all the complaint he made. He died the next day.

She saw no blood on the sheets or pillow, no wound, and no sign of his hair having been cut off. Mr Swayne now questioned her. No-one at the workhouse spoke to her about ill-treatment. She said she told Mr Farr that 'it was reported about that the boy was killed'. She attempted to clarify:

> I told Mr. Farr it was reported about that the boy was killed but I did not tell him any particulars ... I told him what the

boy had said to us ... I told Mr. Farr that I got the report from the common conversation of the village and the people I had been working with. The boy did not say he was killed—he did not say that.

She had spoken to George's brother about it but he did not believe that George had been hurt. He said the master always behaved well to him: 'Charles ... spoke up so plump about the usage to him that we thought it could not be'. He said he had never been ill-used or 'kept short of victuals'. She did say about George:

The boy George was a little obstinate—more than some be— there was not much the matter when he was at home, but the poor thing had suffered a good deal and that had made his temper what it otherwise would not have been.

Mary Clift had said that she visited her nephew with her sister, Elizabeth Rumbold, but it was her sister-in-law, Susannah Thomas, who was now called and said that it was she who had visited George Wheeler with Mrs Clift. She repeated what Mary Clift had said about George telling them that he had been 'thrown' out of bed because he would not get up. Fry had not spoken to her about it. She said that at neither visit did her nephew complain of head wounds or bruises; she never saw a plaister or that his hair had been cut off, and saw no blood on the pillow. Both Mary Clift and Susannah Thomas denied that Fry had told them about the incident, although he had claimed that he told at least one of them, and in the presence of the master. Susannah said that Elizabeth Rumbold was with her and Mary Clift when they saw George the day before he died, and also that they were unable to see George's body on the day of the funeral because the coffin had already been screwed up.

The next witness was Jane Carter. She now lived next door to Susannah Thomas, but was in the workhouse when George Wheeler had died. Examined by Mr Duke, she said that it was her duty to wash George Wheeler's sheets. She never saw blood on his sheets, and never heard any report about George being ill-used. She knew the sheets were those of George Wheeler because Betty Pinkney brought them to her. Betty Pinkney never told her of any ill-usage of the boy. She saw her at Fighledean before she emigrated to Australia.

Responding to questions from Mr Swayne, she said that since she left the workhouse it had been her habit to come back and visit the master and his family: 'I went to see the family because they always behaved so well to me'. She said the master was not rude or rough; he was very kind as were all of his family. She did not come to see any of the other inmates. At this point, Charles Wheeler was recalled and questioned by Mr Swayne. He said that Mr Duke had spoken to him in the street three or four weeks ago, and asked him if the master had not killed his brother, telling him 'not to mention it—he feared he should not get to the end of the story'.

Robert Brown was called. He was in the workhouse at the time that George Wheeler had died but was away on the actual day. He said:

> I heard that Wheeler was bad, but never heard of his ill-usage … I never saw any wound on his head. I never saw his head bound up. I never saw any plaister on his head.

On the behaviour of the master, he had never received any ill-usage from Mr Ralfs, and found no fault in general with the treatment he received in the workhouse. He did say that some of the inmates used Mr Ralfs 'a little rough'.

The last witness called in respect of the charge was Mr John Cape, a sometime guardian living at Idmiston, who had known James Fry for more than twelve years from when he was a crippled boy in the parish. He knew nothing about George Wheeler. He seemed to have been called as a character witness for Fry. Fry never complained to him about ill-usage by the master towards anyone. He said of Fry, 'I don't know much about his character—nothing for or against him'.

Comment on these findings will be reserved until after depositions from several witnesses called to speak to the character of the master and matron, Mr and Mrs Ralfs. The first of these was Mary Dyer. Mary Dyer lived in Salisbury, and had spent two-and-a-half years in the workhouse. Her testimony is quoted at length:

> The Governor's conduct was civility and kindness to the inmates whilst I was in the workhouse. I never knew him to act cruelly to any of the inmates ... [or] heard a report of his having acted cruelly. Since I left the Workhouse I have called on the Governor many times ... He has always been glad to see me and has treated me with kindness.

Regarding the behaviour of the master towards the children:

> If there were any difference in his conduct, he was always more kind to children than other paupers. The children are not afraid of him—quite the reverse. I should not suppose one person in Amesbury could be found to say the Governor was unkind—not if they speak the truth.

She said that she thought that Mrs Ralfs was looking very ill:

> I suppose it is owing to this trouble. I never saw a woman so much altered in my life ... The Governor and the Mrs and the family have been to see me several times at Salisbury. They always appear to take an interest in my welfare. I believe they visit a good many people who have been in the Workhouse, and from what I hear, everyone is glad to see them and speaks well of their kindness. The children used to go to the master every night and shake hands with him and wish him good night and the same to Mrs. ... The children always appear cheerful and I don't believe any of them ever went to bed without kissing the Mrs.

Charles Dyer, Mary's husband, confirmed everything his wife had said. Sarah North, recently widowed, was called next. She also lived in Salisbury and had spent nearly two years in the workhouse. Her sentiments towards the master and his wife were identical to those expressed by the Dyers. Her husband had died in the workhouse:

> He received attention and kindness in the Workhouse. He had everything that was needed for him by the Governor ... Whilst he was able to do it, he spoke of [his] kindness.

Deborah Plummer's testimony was quite touching. She was an inmate of five years, and can also be quoted from at length:

> My father was also an inmate. He died in the Workhouse. He was ill for 12 months. He was formerly paralytic and had no use of his limbs on one side. I waited on him constantly during his illness. The Governor and Matron behaved very kindly to him indeed all the time he was ill up to the time he died. He sometimes had food sent to him from the Governor's table. Father was very pleased and very grateful for the kindness and said so to me ... I have three [children] in the Workhouse, the Governor behaves very kind to them. My children never told me that the Governor and mistress ever behaved unkind to them. I never heard any other child say that the children had been ill-used. When I have been out of the Workhouse I have heard that the Governor and matron behaved more like a father and mother than like a Governor and matron.

Her father had been buried from the workhouse:

> I followed him to the grave. The body was washed and laid out decently. I have seen other examples. There is respect and decency paid to them all. They are never slighted and neglected by the Governor. [He puts] all sorts of flowers that he can get ... round the corpse in the coffin ... when there are none in the Workhouse garden, the Governor sends for them up into the town. There is always a pile on the coffin and the coffin is conveyed to the grave like the coffins of other people in the same rank of life.

The next witness was William May, aged sixty-nine. He lived in Salisbury but had spent a year in the workhouse. He never saw any ill-usage, and was never ill-used himself. He said:

> I have often seen the boys ... [they] went through the old men's
> ward every meal time. They appeared cheerful and contented
> and always very happy I thought.

Two more paupers were called, Maria Green and Ann Perry. Maria Green, who was twenty-four, had been in the workhouse for two years, but was now working as a servant in Salisbury. Her account of the master was also glowing:

> Whilst I was here ... the Governor ... treated me very well
> indeed. I think he endeavoured to make every one comfortable
> in this house and his manner was very kind indeed and so was
> the Mrs. I have been over to see them several times since I left.
> I came over on purpose to see them. I should not have come if
> they had used me ill. I believe they wish to do everyone good
> who has been in the Workhouse. They were very glad to see
> me when I came over, and glad to know I was getting on.

Ann Perry was sixty-seven. She had spent five years in the workhouse, but was now living outside. She said the master and matron treated her and the other paupers with great kindness; when they were sick, the master would send them food from his own table. She nursed the children and the old women, so she had had opportunities of observing the master's kindness first hand:

> The master once gave all the children and nurses a gypsy
> party on the Downs ... we spent the day very joyfully indeed.
> Mrs Ralfs and Mrs Benham [Mrs Ralfs' daughter] went with us.
> We had plenty to eat and drink.

Henry Selfe was called. He was one of the guardians representing the parish of Amesbury. He had visited the workhouse at 'all hours of the day', with and without the master in attendance. He had seen dinner, with food well cooked and served out 'in a decent manner', and : 'the children always appear ... happy and contented'. On the master and matron:

> I have always observed great equanimity of temper in the
> Governor and matron. I never saw any bit of cruelty committed

by [them]. I never heard of the Governor beating the children with severity ... I never had reason to speak to the master about his beating the children. I never heard a report of the master ill-treating the children in any of the villages until I heard of Mr Duke's charges a fortnight ago.

The inmates, including the children, were not reluctant to talk to him during his visits; complaints that had been investigated were invariably found to be frivolous. Henry Selfe was an employer of thirty or forty labourers, so he would, he said, have heard of any stories going round the villages.

The clerk, Richard Wilson, now provided some collateral information from the board minutes regarding some of the witnesses. He confirmed that Mary King had been brought before the board for 'tearing pieces of flesh out of another woman's arm'. On Moses Spreadbury:

He absconded from the Workhouse ... the character then recorded of him is "His character is very bad, a most disaffected pauper, constantly scolding the master and mistress of the house and everybody else that belongs to the establishment".

On James Fry, 'It is stated of him "his character is generally bad"'.

Finally, the chaplain of the workhouse, Rev Fulwar William Fowle, made a long statement to the enquiry. He was a graduate of Merton College, Oxford, a prebend of Salisbury and rural dean, rector of Allington, and was rector of Amesbury from 1817 until 1876. He was about ten years younger than Edward Duke, but had already spent twenty-seven years in Amesbury, so he was well qualified to comment on the activities of the workhouse. He started:

During the time I have been the Chaplain of the Workhouse the conduct of the Governor and matron has been exemplary. Their behaviour to the inmates has been perfectly kind and humane. In no instance have I known them guilty of illtreating or improperly chastising the pauper inmates. Their conduct to the children has been particularly kind. I never knew any instance of unjustifiable severity on the part of the Governor or the matron. I am much about the country and visit all the villages in the neighbourhood—I am particularly called to many of them for being Rural Dean. In no instance have I heard of the paupers having been illtreated or their children chastised improperly by the governor.

When he visited the workhouse, he said that he went to every room and prayed with the inmates. From his diary he confirmed that he visited frequently between 20th March and 17th April 1840. He said he thought he must have been ill between the 5 and 20 March. His curate visited the workhouse on 8 and 15 March 1840. According to Moses Spreadbury, the incident between the master and George Wheeler had taken place on 12 March; Wheeler had been noted by the surgeon as suffering from consumption on 6 April, and died on 17 April. Rev Fowle then made a very interesting observation:

> From the unrestrained way in which ill and dying persons unburden themselves to Clergymen I am confident I should have heard if any ill-treatment had been [taking place] in the Workhouse.

And on George Wheeler:

> I recollect Wheeler perfectly. He never made any complaint to me ... I observed nothing I had seen to support that he was otherwise than tranquil ... during his last illness.

He had observed the 'genial attention' of the master and matron towards sick inmates and great kindness to the children, and 'I have always found the house clean and the inmates, with few exceptions, contented'. The children were happy and contented, cleaner, better fed, and better taught than children in the surrounding villages, and more respectful in their demeanour. The master and matron behaved more like kind parents; the children were not under any duress or fear. He described being out for a drive one day with his wife:

we met a great many children out walking who looked so remarkably clean, happy and healthy that she, not knowing who they were, asked me what children they could be—I answered they are the children of the lowest genders of 23 parishes and that they were coming from the workhouse. I do not know any children of people of this district who could be compared to their general appearance.

He had been present for the four days of the enquiry:

nothing that has transpired has shaken my confidence in the master and matron—that confidence has been confirmed though it did not want that confirmation, for I knew everything that has transpired as well before the investigation as now.

He said he had no reason to doubt James Fry's honesty, although Moses Spreadbury was 'the worst character I have known in the house'. He had refused him communion in consequence of his 'offensive and disturbed character'. Finally:

I wish … to record here what I have said elsewhere that as regards the Governor and the Matron I cannot remember one circumstance in the conduct of the house that I could have wished to be otherwise.

As noted earlier, forty-six persons had made depositions or given evidence, and 100 pages of foolscap notes of that evidence had been taken over four days. Mr Parker must have been exhausted. Nevertheless, within two weeks he had sent the evidence together with some covering remarks to the PLC. One final piece of testimony needs to be considered, and that is the statement made by Charles Ralfs after he had seen the evidence of the enquiry. It was made in the presence of Richard Wilson in his legal capacity as a solicitor.

Ralfs noted the circumstances in which he and his wife were elected master and mistress of the Amesbury Union Workhouse, as well as the subsequent election of his daughters as schoolmistresses. Neither he nor his wife and daughters had ever been reprimanded by the board, nor found fault with by anyone, with the exception of the Rev Edward Duke. Until three years previously, Rev Duke had expressed himself perfectly satisfied with the conduct of the master. However, following a complaint about the board's having left to the discretion of the mistress the procurement of clothing for the inmates:

> from that time to the present, he has not ceased (except in short intervals of illness or absence from home) to find fault with our general management.

It seems that Duke was not only constantly soliciting complaints from the workhouse inmates against the master and his wife, but also talking to the tradespeople in Amesbury regarding their 'movements and proceedings', and 'throwing out insinuations'. Mr Duke would visit the workhouse and spend hours going over the books. Regarding complaints from the inmates,

> this was for some time most paralysing to myself and my wife as we were, when obliged to reprimand any of the inmates for misconduct, whether children or adults, constantly met with "I'll tell Mr Duke of it", but that we are now comparatively free from such annoyance as the inmates, with very few exceptions, are so tired of the repeated interference of Mr Duke that they avoid him if possible.

Ralfs then summarized the outcome of the 1842 enquiry, and his exoneration from any wrongdoing, reproducing the criticism that was made of Duke by the Poor Law Commissioners. The failure of Duke's charges at that time, Ralfs said, only increased his bitterness towards him and his wife. Duke continued to bring charges which were rejected by the board.

Mr Ralfs had found out from Jane Conduit that Duke was about to bring charges against him regarding George Wheeler, and heard from other inmates about the other charges—this before the charges had been brought before the board. Ralfs himself, wishing the charges to be thoroughly investigated, gave Richard Wilson the names of all persons he judged could know anything of the truth or otherwise of the allegations, after Duke had refused to give him or Parker a list of witnesses.

Ralfs now addressed the four charges directly. On Mary King, he declared that he never put anyone in the refractory ward without plenty of dry straw. He thought Mary King had been in there two or three times, but not for the last four years:

> She is an aged and very violent woman, at times hardly knowing what she says or does. Upon one occasion she tore with her nails and fingers another old woman's arms dreadfully.

Regarding the two girls, Ralfs declared that he never hit them with 'rope or rod'. He remembered giving Ann Holmes a box on the ear with his flat hand when he found her crawling on the floor; he couldn't remember boxing Sarah Sainsbury's ear, but said that it was possible.

As for James Coles, Ralfs said 'I declare that I never, to my recollection or belief, struck him with a rope or anything at all'. He had never heard of the wound on Coles' cheek until Duke brought his charge. He had been told subsequently by several of the boys, that it had been administered by John Williams, now deceased. He also denied striking any of the boys in their bedroom.

He recounted the incident involving George Wheeler. Ralfs had come into the ward at 9 or 10 o'clock in the morning to find him still in bed. Although he had lost the use of his 'lower extremities' he was able to dress himself 'almost entirely'. He refused to get dressed. The master then lifted him by the shoulders, not by an arm and leg, placed him on a stool, and then back on the bed. He said he used no 'unnecessary violence' and was not angry or excited. George Wheeler was not hurt, and did not shed tears or shout that he was hurt. Wheeler never subsequently complained to him of having been ill-used, but thanked him and his wife for their kindness to him. The master had never, he said, been reproached by any of the inmates regarding his treatment of George Wheeler, or heard anything about it following the brief 1840 enquiry by the board, until Mr Duke's charges.

Just before Parker's evidence was received by the PLC, another letter was forwarded to Somerset House; this had been sent to Sir James Graham from Gorges Lowther, the chairman of the Amesbury Union guardians. Of all people, after Charles Ralfs and Richard Wilson, Gorges Lowther had probably suffered most from Edward Duke's unremitting persecution of the Amesbury Union and its officers. As chairman, he had had to put up with Duke's constant grievances and points of order, and deal with complaints from the other guardians who were fed up with Duke. He had already written three times to the PLC complaining about Edward Duke's activities, and with the latest charges against the workhouse master he felt that his views, almost certainly reflecting those of all of the guardians, had to be presented to the Home Secretary.

Lowther pointed out that the incident with George Wheeler had been investigated at his instigation shortly after it had happened, the accusation was 'unfounded', and

a mere courtesy from a brother magistrate would have prevented a serious revival of this charge ... without a word of notice to the Board or to me.

This was the third occasion, he said, in which the PLC were involved in investigating Edward Duke's charges against the Amesbury Union and its officers. The first one, involving the integrity of the clerk, had been carried out by Colonel a'Court: 'But so vexatious and malicious did the accusation at once show itself to be, that the proceedings were very soon terminated'. This event does not appear explicitly in the files, but was probably that referred to by a'Court in his letter to Wilson following Duke's letter published in *The Sun* newspaper. Mr Lowther then outlined the investigation carried out by Parker into the twenty-eight charges (twenty-five plus three), again all largely disproved, and outlined the charge against Duke of inciting disobedience in the workhouse, earning him a rebuke from the PLC. Lowther now went on the offensive:

> If your opinion of the validity of these charges is similar to that expressed by the Poor Law Commissioners of the former ones, I trust that you may be pleased to express yourself in terms sufficiently marked to deter Mr Duke from continuing his course of mischievous interference in the details of the management of the workhouse ... which creates continued insubordination, renders the lives of the governor and matron miserable, and makes their duties ... onerous and irksome almost beyond endurance.

And:

> Should you consider the conduct of a person deserving censure who systematically opposes himself to the peaceful working of the law in the house and out of it, by throwing out insinuations the most unjust, by making random and unsupported accusations, by collecting evidence in the most unworthy manner from the least fitting or the most discreditable sources, and should you be of opinion that these charges justly apply to Mr Duke's conduct for a series of years, and emphatically in the commission obtained by him from you, I trust that you will be pleased to express your opinion in a way likely to deter him from continuing his mischievous course.

There can be no doubt of the bitterness felt by Rev Lowther towards his brother clergyman, magistrate, and ex officio guardian.

Henry Walter Parker prefaced the voluminous evidence he had taken, and which he sent to the PLC, with a few remarks (before he saw Ralfs' statement). He mentioned inconsistencies which could not be explained by the lapse of time, in particular the conflicting accounts of the location of the injury to George Wheeler's head.

The only real issue with the old lady, Mary King, seemed to be whether the straw she was given to sleep on in the 'refractory ward' was wet or not. Parker opined that if it was wet, it was possibly because of the cup of water the old lady had thrown at the master. The incident with the two girls, Sainsbury and Holmes, he dismissed as the most trivial occurrence. The boy Coles, it seems *had* been beaten and his face cut open, not by the master, but by the old schoolmaster, John Williams, now deceased. Parker commented on the confusion arising because some of the paupers called Ralfs 'The Governor' and some 'The Master'.

On the alleged cruelty to George Wheeler, it seemed that Fry and Spreadbury, for reasons known to themselves, had conspired to fabricate a story from the fairly trivial event of George Wheeler's refusal to get dressed one morning. Parker commented on workhouse inmates who were 'turbulent and mischievous, some who are imbecile or with intellects weakened by sickness or other causes'.

The evidence from the aunts, Parker did not mention and appeared to discount. The overwhelming evidence from all the other witnesses, including an eye witness, was not only that Wheeler did *not* suffer injury at the master's hands, but that he was most grateful to him for his kindness, this gratitude being expressed on the very last day of his life.

The master and 'matron' of the workhouse, Parker said, were 'kind, attentive, and considerate', and had the 'good opinion' of the guardians and the 'respect' of the poor.

The PLC's response was drafted on 22 May. The report was signed by an assistant secretary, 'W. G. L.' The charges were summarized, as was the evidence given in respect of each charge. For each incident, the likely truth of what had actually happened was detailed, given the weight of evidence for and against. In the case of George Wheeler, the case against the master 'was not substantiated in any way', notwithstanding the inconsistencies in the evidence referred to by Parker. On the boy Coles, the evidence showed quite clearly that the blow was inflicted not by the master, but by the pauper schoolmaster. The charge that the master beat the two girls with a rope was found to be wholly false. The charge involving Mary King was 'not substantiated'.

The Poor Law Commissioners were masters of equivocation, as can be seen from their many previous communications, and perhaps with an eye to possible publicity—the leaking of the report to the press—they found that the guardians of the Amesbury Union and its master were not wholly exonerated from an element of fault. If, during the 1840 enquiry by the board into George Wheeler's death, the guardians had thought to include his relatives either as witnesses or observers, it seemed to the PLC likely that rumours of wrongdoing on the part of the master would never have started.

The fact that a pauper schoolmaster had beaten one of the boys with a rope severely enough to badly cut his cheek, pointed to the dangers of employing paupers to teach the children. The charge of beating the two girls with a rope was false, although:

> The commissioners do not mean to say that the master was justified in thus hastily striking these two girls; such a mode of correction is forbidden by workhouse rules and is objectionable in itself as being open to great abuse.

On Mary King:

> After this lapse of time, and with a different set of regulations in force, it seems hardly necessary to enter into the question whether the master was strictly justified in placing Mary King in the Refractory Ward on his own authority. It is sufficiently evident that his conduct was free from the harshness imputed to him.

Having used seven pages to detail its judgement on the charges, the PLC used six more to reproduce at length the evidence from the one-time pauper Mary Dyer, and the chaplain Rev Fowle, which extolled the virtues of the master and Mrs Ralfs and their kindness to the children. The obvious intent of the PLC was to demonstrate that after so much negative publicity for workhouses in general, the Amesbury Workhouse at least was as far different from the one portrayed in *Oliver Twist* as it was possible to be. Not only that; in their earlier remarks the PLC wanted it to be quite clear that they were enforcing the workhouse rules rigorously, and would treat any infringement very seriously.

In the event, the 1844 enquiry at the Amesbury Union was *not* leaked to the press, and not a single word about it ever appeared in the newspapers.

# Aftermath

Given the evidence presented to Mr Parker and reported by him to the PLC, the acquittal of the master by the latter from the four charges is entirely unsurprising. On the other hand what is most surprising, is that Mr Duke thought that the flimsy evidence he had collected, much of it hearsay, justified his serious charges.

Duke had heard rumours of Mary King's treatment but 'could not remember where'. He interviewed her daughter and granddaughter but not her, and based his charge on what they told him. The daughter referred him to the wife of James Coles regarding evidence of two girls having been beaten with a rope. Mrs Coles allegedly told him that she and her daughter had seen the master beating two girls with a rope, and saw the marks on their shoulders and arms afterwards. But in cross-examination, she admitted only seeing a girl with red marks on her shoulders and not seeing any beating at all. And her name was Mrs 'Cool' or 'Coole' not Coles, and her husband's name was William not James. Mr Duke did not speak to the girls in question.

The boy who had received the cut cheek was named Cole or Coles, and Duke having heard, as he thought, a rumour from Mrs London, spoke to the boy. In this case at least, Mr Duke may have been led astray by what the boy told him, since Coles prevaricated during cross-examination as noted by Parker. It is also clear that Duke became thoroughly confused over the names.

The most serious charge, that of physical assault on the crippled boy George Wheeler arose, Mr Duke thought, from a rumour he had heard from Mrs London, although she denied that it was from her. He interviewed three witnesses, but Moses Spreadbury was blind, and his mind was clearly disturbed, and John Pothecary, who was also an eye-witness, denied that anything other than the boy being removed from the bed by the master had occurred. There was no crying out, he said, very little if any blood, and no plaister. Only James Fry claimed to have seen the boy's head gashed open.

Mr Duke was a magistrate of considerable experience, as he kept reminding people, but he should have been very well versed in the practice of hearing evidence and getting witnesses' names correct, bearing in mind the flexible nature of spelling at the time. Likewise, he should have been able to judge whether he was being told the truth, particularly from the 'labouring classes' with whom he had had much contact in court, and should have cross-checked if he suspected that he wasn't. There was also the fact that the George Wheeler incident had already been investigated by the board, and minuted, that minute having been read out in Duke's presence. If Mr Duke had thought to consult Gorges Lowther or Richard Wilson before making his charge, he might have had that pointed out to him.

Several of the witnesses had said that Mr Duke was constantly asking the workhouse inmates whether they had any complaints, and some of them criticised him for it. Was he deliberately led on a wild goose chase by paupers exasperated with him? Equally likely, he was so blinded by his determination to prove some wrongdoing by the workhouse master, union officers, or the other guardians, that his judgement and common sense entirely failed him. It is also possible that his illnesses had caused confusion and memory lapses in respect of who had told him what and when.

The charges he brought in respect of Mary King and the two girls were entirely demolished by the supposed victims themselves. James Coles lied during the enquiry and almost certainly lied to Mr Duke, but several witnesses had stated what had really happened, that it was the old schoolmaster, now dead, who had beaten Coles with a rope and cut his face.

The critical charge, in respect of George Wheeler, was enquired into in the most minute detail by Mr Parker. Apart from Edward Duke himself, nineteen witnesses were called to give evidence regarding the truth or otherwise of the allegation that the master had assaulted George Wheeler, and that this had led to his premature death. Duke's two primary witnesses were James Fry and Moses Spreadbury. Fry claimed that the master had seized the boy by an arm and leg, threw him on the floor, then picked him up and threw him on the bed, where he cut the back of his head on the flint wall. He said the boy cried out and there was blood on the pillow. He also said that, at his request, the doctor had put a plaister on the back of the boy's head and that Betty Pinkney had washed the wound and cut the hair back with a pair of scissors. The boy was in very bad health afterwards, and died five weeks later. Moses Spreadbury, who was blind, said he heard the boy cry "Murder!" He came into the room and spoke to George Wheeler who was sobbing and crying. The boy told him that the master had thrown him out of bed, that he should not live six weeks, and that he, Spreadbury, should 'publish it', i.e. tell everyone what the master had done.

But Abraham Joules, another cripple in the sick ward, also saw what happened. He said the master simply 'drawed' the boy out of bed and 'put' him on the floor; the boy cried out but he could not make out what he said. He saw no blood to 'signify'. No-one cut his hair with scissors and no-one put a plaister on his head. John Pothecary's account matched with Abraham Joules, although he said the boy had a small scratch on his forehead. Charles Kilford, another inmate, also crippled, came into the ward just after the so-called incident. He had heard the master talking to George Wheeler. When he asked George what had happened, he had said that the master had 'thrown him out of bed' because he would not get up. The boy did not cry murder but 'oh dear'. There was no wound, no blood from his nose and ears, and none on the pillow or sheet. George Wheeler's brother Charles, who visited his brother several times a day, never saw a bruise, wound, plaister, or hair cut off, and never saw blood on the sheets or pillows. Jane Conduit never saw a wound, or plaister, or hair that had been cut off. Jane Carter, who washed George Wheeler's sheets, never saw any blood on any of them. Charles Pyle, the medical officer, never treated George Wheeler for a wound or applied a plaister to him. He had treated the boy for consumption, so he saw him regularly. He never saw blood on the wall or pillow. Furthermore, a number of witnesses, including his brother, said that George had frequently expressed his gratitude to the master for the way he was looked after.

The only evidence that the master really had assaulted George Wheeler, came from James Fry who claimed that he had seen it happen, Moses Spreadbury, who although blind, said that he heard the boy cry 'murder', and on asking what was wrong, was told by the boy that the master had assaulted him, and two of the boy's aunts, who said that George had told them that the master had 'used him ill'. Fry had stated in evidence that his vision was defective and had been so for a year, although that was not commented on in Parker's report to the PLC. Possibly Fry was mistaken in what he claimed to have seen; more likely he had manufactured the story for his own reasons, presumably to make trouble for the master. Spreadbury's doubtful sanity, and the fact that he was blind, would surely have discounted his testimony.

The evidence of the aunts, which Parker had not mentioned in his report, was a little more problematic. They said that on their second visit George had told them that he had been 'used very ill'. 'He' had thrown him out of bed because he would not get up.* The 'he' they assumed was the master. But was it Elizabeth Rumbold or Susannah Thomas (or both) who had accompanied Mary Clift on the first visit to their nephew? Fry had said that two women used to visit. All three were there on the second visit, but that had been the day before George Wheeler died and he must have been very weak then. Did they mishear him, or exaggerate a passing comment? Did they hear what they wanted to hear having already heard rumours? They claimed that they had not spoken to Fry, although he insisted that he had told two of them of the incident, one in front of the master. That George Wheeler had been removed from bed by the master was not in doubt; the issue was, whether it had been done with violence.

It was Mary Clift who had brought the incident to the attention of the guardians in the first place, and as George Wheeler's closest adult relations, his aunts deserved to have their testimony considered. Evidently Parker chose to disregard it, probably because it amounted to what the aunts said George had told them on one single occasion. They said he had told them that he had been 'used ill', but that conflicted with the evidence of virtually everyone else who had had day-to-day contact with their nephew over the several weeks leading up to his death.

When the testimony of the character of Charles Ralfs and his wife was added to the wealth of evidence that George Wheeler was not assaulted by the master, many might conclude that Duke's charges were fantasy. Witness after witness deposed to the kindness of the master and his wife, particularly to the children. He frequently sent the sick paupers food from his own table, and a number of inmates who had left

---

* Charles Kilford also claimed Wheeler told him the master had 'thrown him out of bed', but Kilford had arrived immediately after the incident, and said that the boy did not cry out, and was not distressed. George Wheeler may have been using idiomatic language, rather than suggesting that he was actually *thrown* out of bed.

the workhouse returned time after time to visit the Ralfses. Mr Ralfs organised a picnic on the downs for the children with plenty to eat and drink, and the children would shake hands with the master and kiss Mrs Ralfs before going to bed—one witness described the master and his wife as more like a father and mother than master and matron. And when paupers died, Mr Ralfs sometimes paid for flowers for their funerals.

And what of Mr Duke? He had effectively staked his reputation on these charges, and notwithstanding the equivocation of the Poor Law Commissioners, his allegations were found to be without foundation. Given the almost universal approbation of the pauper inmates for the master, it is quite difficult to understand Duke's motivation for persecuting him. In his statement, Ralfs said that Duke's campaign against him and his wife commenced around three years previously. In fact it was in 1842 that Duke had charged the master with not providing the pauper children with an adequate change of stockings. The PLC had acknowledged that this was contrary to the rules, but the guardians had flatly refused to reprimand him. This had led to Parker's first enquiry at Amesbury, when Mr Duke's twenty-five or twenty-eight charges against all and sundry were found, with one minor exception, to be without foundation. Perhaps it was that event that motivated Duke.

It is notable that the PLC in its report on Parker's enquiry into George Wheeler, and unlike the previous occasion, made no mention of Mr Duke other than that it was he who had brought the charges. There was no censure of his activities, so as far as he was concerned, nothing had materially changed. He was still a magistrate and able to continue as an ex officio guardian of the Amesbury Union. Gorges Lowther, in his letter to the Home Secretary had been quite explicit that Duke should be 'deter[red] … from continuing his mischievous course'.

Mr Duke could have been expelled as a magistrate, but after all had he really done anything bad enough to warrant such an extreme move? He had certainly been most indiscreet when he suggested to the paupers that in their place he would have refused to work in the washhouse without an allowance of beer. But that had happened two years previously and had been very publicly aired at the time—including in the newspapers. If anything were to be done, it should have been done then. The letter of Gorges Lowther to Sir James Graham, and Charles Ralfs' statement, detailed Duke's systematic 'mischief', and there is little doubt that he made the lives of Mr and Mrs Ralfs and Richard Wilson a misery. But it could be argued that he was simply acting out of an extreme, if misguided, sense of duty. A public expulsion might well have branded Duke a martyr, and could have rebounded on all concerned in an entirely unintended way. Nevertheless, given the strength of feeling in the Amesbury Union against Duke, it seems probable that he could have been forced to step down. In fact, his name appeared in the magistracy lists for Wiltshire in the following year, 1845, so he was quite definitely not expelled from the bench at that time.

But from the date of the 1844 enquiry, Mr Duke's magisterial activities abruptly stop; the 13 April 1844 Quarter Sessions at Salisbury was his last appearance, and on that occasion he resigned from the chairmanship of the 'second court'. As well as that, he also ceased playing any part in the guardianship of the Amesbury Union. He is mentioned in the minute book in an entry following the PLC's verdict on Parker's report; the original is missing, but a copy was forwarded to the PLC on 4 June 1844. It was a unanimous resolution passed the previous day at an extraordinary meeting of the Amesbury Union guardians. It read:

> The Guardians of this union have long seen with much regret the malignant spirit shown by the Rev Edward Duke against the master and mistress of the Amesbury Workhouse, more

particularly evinced in the recent charges made by him to
the Secretary of State of cruelty to the inmates which having
been investigated by Mr Parker one of the assistant Poor Law
Commissioners and proved to be totally false.

It went on:

> The Guardians take this opportunity of expressing their
> satisfaction and confidence in the conduct of the Master
> and Mistress and highly commend their kind and humane
> treatment of the paupers in this house on all occasions and
> they cannot too strongly condemn Mr Duke for having brought
> forward charges seriously affecting Mr Ralfs' character which
> he had not one tittle of evidence to support and by doing so
> disgraced himself as a magistrate and shewn a malevolent
> and unchristian feeling highly unbecoming to the profession
> to which he belongs.

Perhaps the emotional relief felt by the clerk, Richard Wilson,
was responsible for his uncharacteristic lapse in punctuation
and sentence structure.

If Mr Duke had resigned as a guardian there is no way
to check the fact directly, since the minute book for 1844 is
missing, and such an event would certainly have been recorded.
However, it would also have been notified to the PLC, and Mr
Duke's name ceases to appear in the correspondence that
passed between the Amesbury Union and the PLC from the
date of Wilson's letter. A resignation would, in any case, have
been a pointless exercise. By the 1834 Act, as long as Mr Duke
was a magistrate, he could be, whether anybody liked it or not,
and whether he acted upon it or not, an ex officio guardian of
the Amesbury Union.

Thereafter, Mr Duke largely disappears from mention
in the newspapers also. There were some articles and
advertisements for his 1846 book on the *Druidical Temples
of Wilts*, and mention of his '20-foot-high blooming aloe'.
He appeared on a committee for a 'Salisbury and Swindon'
extension of a railway, he presided over a marriage ceremony

or two, and a woman reportedly hanged herself after attending one of his sermons in Salisbury. One of his last outings in the press, was a report that he appeared on the platform during a meeting against John Henry Newman's 'Tractarian revival of Popery'.

What may have happened is that a confidential word was said to him, possibly by the Lord Chancellor, to the effect that if he quietly withdrew from active duty, no more would be said; he and his family would be spared public disgrace. It was in no-one's interest to have a scandal. If Mr Duke had been publicly dismissed from the magistracy, details of Parker's enquiry would almost certainly have come out. Although Ralfs was entirely exonerated, questions would be asked and scrutiny from the press and elsewhere might well cause further trouble. Fry and Spreadbury would have been only too pleased to have their views disseminated in public.

Mr Duke's ill health might also have played a part in his retirement. Perhaps his doctor, possibly Dr Pyle from the union, advised him that given the state of his health, he would not survive a public scandal. Whatever inducements were used he acceded to them, and elected to spend the rest of his days developing his grand theory to explain the origins of Silbury Hill, Avebury and Stonehenge.

# *Epilogue*

Whether by choice or duress Mr Duke had retired from public life, and his mainly literary activities after May 1844 have been covered in an earlier chapter. Gorges Lowther, Richard Wilson, and the Ralfses, along with the other guardians at the Amesbury Union, must have breathed a considerable sigh of relief. Now at last, the demanding affairs of the union could be conducted without the constant and destructive interference of the Reverend Edward Duke.

It can be assumed that Mr Duke did take more than a little pleasure the following year in reading the newspaper accounts of events at the Andover Workhouse. Andover was the adjacent union, and Duke's nemesis, Henry Walker Parker, was a fairly prominent casualty. Details of what happened there have been covered in Ian Anstruther's book, *The Scandal of the Andover Workhouse*. Reduced to its basics, the master at Andover was a drunken and lustful embezzler of workhouse resources. The inmates were so poorly fed, that they were reduced to sucking the marrow out of putrid bones sent to the workhouse to be crushed for fertilizer. There was an enquiry led by Mr Parker which was deemed unsatisfactory by the PLC, and Parker was forced to resign his post. A subsequent and very public parliamentary enquiry led eventually to the disbanding of the Poor Law Commission itself. Mr Duke must have been jubilant, but apparently he made no public utterances on the subject.

Edward Duke died at Lake House on 28 August 1852, and was buried with his ancestors in the parish church of Wilsford-cum-Lake. There is a substantial memorial to him and his wife on the wall to the left of the altar:

IN A VAULT

WITH HIS FOREFATHERS BENEATH THIS CHURCH

REST THE MORTAL REMAINS

OF

EDWARD DUKE, CLERK, M.A.,

OF LAKE HOUSE.

AS A MAGISTRATE AND UPRIGHT MAN

HE WAS WIDELY KNOWN THROUGH

THE COUNTY OF WILTS;

AND WAS BELOVED BY HIS FAMILY

AND BY THE INHABITANTS OF THIS PARISH.

BORN AUGUST 24TH 1779,

DECEASED AUGUST 28TH 1852.


ALSO OF HARRIET, HIS WIFE,

DAUGHTER OF HENRY HINXMAN,

OF IVY-CHURCH HOUSE, ESQUIRE,

BORN SEPTEMBER 1ST 1788,

DECEASED APRIL 25TH 1873


Their initials are engraved on a flagstone immediately in front of the chancel, indicating that the remains lie below in the most exalted place in the church.

In reviewing the various accounts of Edward Duke's activities, his literary and antiquarian ambitions, his time on the bench, and his service as a Poor Law guardian, it is next to impossible to discern what motivated him to act in the way that he did, particularly in respect of the Amesbury Union. Was he simply an over-enthusiastic philanthropist genuinely concerned with the well-being of the poor—a man on a crusade to carry out his duties as a Poor Law guardian absolutely to the letter of the law and beyond? Was he, again to quote Alexander Solzhenitsyn, 'that one righteous person, without whom ... no city can stand—nor the world'? Or was he, as his peers would quite likely have insisted, a petty, grievance-hunting pest, totally lacking in common sense, judgement, and what was practical, and unaware of the principles of expediency and compromise?

Mr Duke was a very experienced magistrate, or rather, he had been on the bench for nearly thirty years, yet the evidence he presented to the critically important 1844 enquiry at Amesbury was highly unprofessional. It was also extraordinarily indiscreet to discuss his intentions with various of the workhouse inmates before Ralfs or any of the guardians had been informed. For his most serious charge against the workhouse master, Duke had just one witness, James Fry, who claimed to have seen the governer assaulting George Wheeler. Fry's evidence was contradicted by virtually every other witness, at least one of whom, Abraham Joules, also an eyewitness whom Duke had interviewed, claimed that no assault had taken place. Anyone with a real concern for justice would have spoken to some of the other witnesses, not to mention his brother guardians, before bringing such a serious indictment. Much of Duke's other evidence seemed to have been based on rumour and hearsay. He couldn't remember who had told him what, and he got the names of the witnesses wrong. He claimed in his deposition that they had said things which they later denied when cross-examined, and he acted like a spoiled child when he refused to supply Mr Parker with a list of his witnesses.

It may be that Mr Duke saw himself as a latter-day Socrates; according to Plato, Socrates had said at his trial:

> [I] am a sort of gadfly, given to the state by God ... all day long and in all places ... always fastening upon you, arousing and persuading and reproaching you.

Mr Duke would have known his Plato and would have been familiar with the *Dialogues*, where Socrates is described as constantly questioning and probing the status quo and received wisdom in Athens—and being quite regularly insulted for his trouble. But Socrates was a master of logical enquiry, and Edward Duke was far too hasty and petulant for logic to play much part in his behaviour. Perhaps he had Socrates in mind when he told the Home Secretary that he would prefer to go to prison rather than allow Parker to conduct the 1844 enquiry; but when his bluff was called, he gave in without a murmur.

Time after time Duke wrote to the PLC with a whole series of complaints. He repeated complaints that had already been dealt with and seemed to forget others that he had made previously. He made the lives of the officers of the union truly intolerable. It is no wonder that the guardians crowded around Parker after the 1842 enquiry congratulating him.

Mr Duke's performance at the Quarter Sessions in respect of the new assize court at Devizes was particularly extraordinary. At Amesbury he had described himself on one occasion as standing up to 'the united and clamorous voices of the many combined against the one'. It seemed to be a recurring theme for him. He was also most cavalier with the courtesies and protocols due to brother magistrates, Ludlow Bruges in particular, yet he became very upset and petulant, resorting to open letters, when the tables were turned on him. Then there was the very serious charge that he made against the prison governor at Devizes, based solely on information received from a prisoner convicted of a capital offence. That surely demonstrated Mr Duke's pathological failure of judgement.

A psychologist reading this account of Mr Duke might be able to diagnose his mental state. Possibly, his two books might help. There is little evidence in *Prolusiones*, and none at all in *Druidical Temples*, of any external editorial control. Both books are written in the style of a conversation with the reader, and the unexpurgated workings of Duke's brain are very clearly on show. In both books he wanders off at tangents, his ideas emerging in a sort of stream of consciousness.

It may be that the trauma of the 1844 enquiry and Mr Duke's probably enforced retirement afterwards caused him to have a mental breakdown. That might explain many of the oddities in the later book, particularly his inexplicable volte-face on the involvement of the Druids in Stonehenge, and his astronomical and geometrical howlers. Perhaps he was encouraged to produce the 1846 book as therapy, and simply cut and pasted bits from the newspaper series with no clear vision of an outline, having forgotten his previous conclusions. It could be seen as evidence of the 'decay of [his] faculties' mentioned in one of his obituaries.

Undoubtedly Duke suffered from paranoia and delusions of grandeur; he was constantly reminding his correspondents that he was owed respect as a gentleman from one of the oldest families in the county, and was a magistrate of thirty years' experience. But he was also a charitable man, always concerning himself with individual cases of hardship in his locality. He was supposed never to have spoken a harsh word to anyone in his household, and yet he carried on a vindictive programme of persecution over several years against the master and mistress of the Amesbury workhouse. They were persons of social rank and resource considerably below his own, and virtually powerless to defend themselves against him.

Mr Duke seems destined to remain forever an enigma; certainly he was a person of such extraordinary and inexplicable temperament, that hardly two or even three of Charles Dickens' most bizarre creations combined would do justice to his character and behaviour.

Charles Ralfs had served as the master of the Amesbury workhouse for eight years by the time he was acquitted in the 1844 enquiry. He was to spend his remaining time there under far happier circumstances, and died in harness at the age of sixty-eight. On 27 June 1853, Richard Wilson reported Ralfs' death earlier that morning—without further comment—to the meeting of the guardians. Immediately after the Duke affair nine years earlier, the guardians had unanimously agreed that they 'highly commend [the master and mistress] for their kind and humane treatment of the paupers in this house on all occasions'. However there was no similar motion following the master's death, and this seems somewhat less than generous considering his undoubted conscientiousness in his role, as well as the misery he had suffered under Duke's persecution. A brief notice of his death in a newspaper did state that he was 'much respected by all who knew him'. Mrs Ralfs fared little better; having been asked for a testimonial since she was obliged to leave the workhouse after her husband's death, the guardians declared that 'Mrs Amelia Ralfs has filled the situation of matron ... to the entire satisfaction of the Board of Guardians'. Perhaps this matter of fact treatment was the inevitable lot of employees drawn from the 'lower orders'.

Gorges Lowther also died in harness, but the reaction of the guardians could not have been more different. His death came in 1881 but as late as 28 April 1880, when he was 88 years old, he was again unanimously elected chairman of the guardians, even though the last time he had attended a meeting had been January 1879. The 1881 census described him still as rector of Orcheston St George, a post he had occupied for more than fifty years. When he died a few weeks later, the guardians resolved unanimously that:

> This [newly elected] Board at their first meeting cannot commence their business without recording their regret at the death of Mr Lowther, who ever since the formation of the Union in 1835, now a period of 45 years, has been elected their chairman and whose capacity for business and unvarying courtesy of demeanour may be equalled but never will be surpassed by any who may succeed him.

Lowther was enormously respected by all. The only person present at the meeting who had been there at the inception of the union was the clerk, Richard Wilson, who recorded the resolution and probably authored it.

Wilson himself remained in his job at the Amesbury Union for another two years when he too died, apparently quite suddenly. He was replaced by his son, R A Wilson. As with Gorges Lowther, the board expressed its regret:

> The guardians of this Board desire to express their deep sense of the loss they have sustained by the death of their clerk Mr R M Wilson who had filled the office to the great satisfaction of the Board and to his own credit since its formation in October 1835.

Wilson had also been county coroner, and in 1877 he was mayor of Salisbury.

It is notable that for more than forty-five years, Lowther and Wilson had worked tirelessly on the repetitively tedious and thankless task of overseeing the welfare of the most disadvantaged persons in the community. They were paid for the work, but nevertheless it is an enormous credit to them both that even with the almost unendurable presence of Mr Duke for nine of those years, they had carried on regardless. They were true public servants.

Henry Walter Parker, Mr Duke's arch-enemy, endured a difficult few years following the 1844 enquiry. In 1849 he emigrated to Australia where he enjoyed a career as solicitor and barrister, and earned a glowing obituary when he died in 1874. Following the PLC's dissatisfaction with his handling of the 1845 enquiry at the Andover Union, he was pressured to resign. He was sufficiently upset with his treatment, that he published the extensive correspondence he had had with the Home Secretary, Sir James Graham, in an attempt to convince the Bar that he had been shabbily treated and was competent to continue to practise law. When the parliamentary select committee enquiry reported on the Andover affair in 1846, among other things it noted that notwithstanding Parker's 'defective superintendence' at Andover, the PLC's treatment of him had been 'irregular and arbitrary'.

Three years later Parker emigrated, still a very bitter man despite the apparent recognition of his unfair dismissal. His admittedly questionable performance at Andover is a matter of record and it was not the only time he had courted controversy. *The Times* had reported in 1841 that Parker had recommended Joseph Howe for the post of master of the Eton Union. Howe had previously been implicated in the death by scalding of a boy at the Brackley Union. The master was subsequently fined and dismissed from the Eton Union for confining a female pauper in an unheated room without bedclothes or a 'convenience' for twenty-four hours, an event quite similar to one of Mr Duke's charges at Amesbury.

It is interesting to speculate how the actions of Mr Parker at Andover might have been influenced by the Amesbury affair. At Amesbury, the accusations against the workhouse master were intimately dissected, only to be roundly dismissed as being without foundation. The evidence was very clear, and there was no question that Parker could have influenced the outcome of the enquiry, regardless of his past record and any subsequent taint from future events. It is not impossible that the findings at Amesbury may have coloured his general attitude towards allegations against workhouse masters, and could have affected his judgement at Andover.

As a consequence of the select committee report on the Andover affair, the PLC was fatally damaged; it was finally dissolved in 1847 to be replaced by the Poor Law Board. The PLC was hopelessly unfit for purpose, as is clear from some of the responses to communications from both Duke and the Amesbury guardians, as well as the way Mr Parker was dismissed. Mr Duke must have greeted the news of its demise with not a little satisfaction, and the irony of the situation is worthy of comment. For at least seven years, as the tenor of Duke's communications to the commissioners became more and more fractious and disruptive, the PLC did virtually nothing to rectify the situation. Time after time the commissioners responded with the most anodyne answers, sometimes providing a response of sorts while stressing that the view was not binding in law. Frequently the question was turned back to the Amesbury guardians, and on at least one occasion when this was done, it was quite clear that no-one at the PLC had actually bothered to read Duke's letter in any detail. Mr Duke had prayed for the PLC's 'extinction', but for quite different reasons from the ones that led to its eventual dissolution.

The Amesbury Union Workhouse continued as such until the 1930s, when it was re-designated a 'Public Assistance Institution'. The buildings were demolished thirty years later, but I recall visiting them with my father in the early 1960s when they were in ruins. As we walked through the various rooms I remember kicking the flints from which they had been constructed, and which littered the floor. I wondered whether one of those we saw might have been responsible for George Wheeler's death—being quite sure at the time, as my father believed, that that is what had happened.

A brief obituary of Mr Duke in the Linnean Society magazine outlined his life, adding only that he had a valuable and extensive library containing 'every Wiltshire author he could obtain'. The *Gentleman's Magazine* devoted a page to Mr Duke. It mentioned his books and the correspondence he had carried on in its pages. It also mentioned his 'firmness and decision of public character' as a magistrate, and his personal behaviour, '[never] to have spoken an unkind word to a member of his family or household'. Neither obituary mentioned that he had been a guardian of the Amesbury Union. The *Salisbury and Wiltshire Journal* carried a memorial in which his achievements were somewhat exaggerated, particularly his relationship with Sir Richard Colt Hoare. It also said that he was a fellow of the Royal Society—he wasn't. It said he was 'Chairman of the Bench of County Magistrates'—he wasn't, although he did, apparently, chair the 'second court' at the Sessions. It too, made no mention of his time as a Poor Law guardian, but it did throw some light on the state of his health, mentioning the 'gradual decay of the reverend gentleman's faculties for some time past'. A later account of his life in *Wiltshire Worthies* did recall his Poor Law activities, where it was said that his conduct 'raised him up opponents, but none could impugn the honesty and goodness of his intentions'. When the legend becomes fact, print the legend.

History has been somewhat kinder to Mr Duke than he might have deserved. He has an entry in the *Oxford Dictionary of National Biography* where his principal claim to fame is that he was an 'antiquary', a title that his achievements in that area hardly warrant. His book, *Druidical Temples*, is described briefly. There is no word of the disputes with his fellow magistrates or of his grievance-hunting 'gadfly' activities at the Amesbury Union. It is notable that none of the contemporary obituaries mention his Poor Law guardianship. His abrupt departure in

1844 and the reasons for it may, after all, have been known of in journalistic circles, although nothing was ever published. Perhaps it was decided not to sully his reputation, and allow his misdemeanours to be laid to rest with him.

Mr Duke's books are now largely forgotten, although *Druidical Temples* is occasionally referenced in works on Stonehenge, mainly to illustrate the lunatic theories that arise from attempts to understand that most enigmatic of monuments.

## Appendix 1
### The Poor Laws

Formal provision for the poor existed in England well before the Norman Conquest. Giving alms to the poor was and still is a duty within the Judeo-Christian and Islamic traditions, and Egbert, Archbishop of York in the eighth century, determined by an ordinance that the poor should receive one third of the parish tithes; 'exactly such a division was confirmed, in the eleventh century, by a law of Ethelred'. But by the end of the fifteenth century this arrangement had effectively ceased.

Gradually the parish became a local governing body, with householders meeting in the church, 'in vestry assembled', presided over by the vicar or rector, with its executive officers, the churchwardens, chosen from the householders. And in the words of the Webbs:

> Upon this spontaneously arising local governing body in each parish, which soon assumed unchallenged power to levy rates upon the parishioners, the King and Parliament, from the beginning of the sixteenth century onwards, imposed successive civil functions.

Part of these rates were used for the relief of the poor, and these could be added to by charitable bequests from wealthy parishioners. Parishes were also able to subsidize support for their poor using revenue generated from the church or parish 'stock'. Livestock gifted to the parish was used to generate income for the benefit of the poor, and this could be further enhanced by holding a 'church ale'. The ale was an outdoor celebration, a fair or fete, including music and dancing, usually held near Whitsuntide. Announcements from the pulpits of neighbouring parishes urged attendance. Grain for brewing into ale, and meat, eggs, butter, cheese, and other foodstuffs were donated to the parish for purchase at the ale, the proceeds going to the benefit of the church stock. Unfortunately, the 'drunkenness ... occasional disorder and ... boisterous joviality' of the ale attracted the notice of the Puritans; towards the end of the sixteenth century ales became less and less common and were even suppressed.

In the towns and cities the Corporations provided further poor relief and set up hospitals, alms houses, and schools, assisted by the merchant and craft guilds.

The poor could also expect support from the monasteries. There were around a thousand of these in England up to the time of the Dissolution; almost nowhere in the country was further than one or two hours' walk away from an order of 'monks, nuns, friars, [or] knights' committed to support the poor of the neighbourhood. By the time of the Dissolution though,

> monastic zeal and monastic charity had "grown cold"; and ... some of the wealthiest of these establishments made "a very scanty show of almsgiving" in proportion to their income.

Furthermore, by the fifteenth century there was a feeling that the indiscriminate charity dispensed was doing more harm than good. Thus support for the poor was organized *ad hoc*, and entirely at local level. And as noted by the Webbs:

> The King, his Council and his Parliament, were enacting and carrying out laws relating to the poor of a character exactly opposite to that of the almsgiving medieval church.

Initially, Parliament's only concern with the poor was to pass legislation to force the able-bodied to work, control begging and vagrancy, and outlaw the giving of alms to those able to work. In 1531, an Act was passed whereby 'aged poor and impotent persons' would be provided by magistrates with a letter authorizing them to beg within a certain area. Anyone begging outside of their appointed area would suffer two days in the stocks, and those found begging without a letter would be stripped to the waist and flogged. In 1536, the 1531 Act was repealed and replaced with 'An Act for Punishment of sturdye Vacabundes and Beggers', which finally mandated care for the poor. 'Officers' at city, borough, or parish level were required to 'socour, fynde, and keep all and every the same poore people by way of voluntarie and charitable almes', as well as ensuring that 'sturdie vacabunde[s]' were set to work.

Other legislation followed, but the most significant development was the passing of 'An Act for the Relief of the Poor', 1601, during the last years of the reign of Queen Elizabeth I. This introduced a formal structure of poor relief to be administered at parish level. Parish officers—churchwardens and overseers—as well as some ratepayers, appointed by at least two magistrates, levied a poor rate from the 'Occupier[s] of Lands' within the parish, and this was used to provide assistance in cash and kind to the needy. This parish executive subsequently became known as a 'select vestry', and consisted of important members of the parish—senior ratepayers and parish officials, usually including the minister. Exactly when the term came into use is not clear, but there was an Act of 1663, during the reign of Charles II, for 'regulating Select Vestryes'.

The Relief of the Poor Act went further than just collecting a tax and handing out relief; it introduced a structure to find gainful employment for the able-bodied poor and their children. In the case of adults, the parish was required to provide 'a convenient stock of flax, hemp, wool, thread, iron, and other necessary ware and stuff, to set the poor on work'. Manufactured product would be sold to subsidize the poor rate. Children were to be bound as apprentices—males until the age of twenty-four; females to the age of twenty-one or until such time as they were married.

The parents and grandparents of the poor and the infirm were obliged, if able, to support them. For the 'impotent poor', those unable to work, the 'old, blind [and] lame', the parish was required

> to erect, build and set up in fit and convenient Places of
> Habitation, in such Waste or Common, at the general Charges
> of the Parish or otherwise of the Hundred or County as
> aforesaid, to be taxed, rated and gathered in Manner before
> expressed, convenient Houses of Dwelling for the said
> impotent Poor; and also to place Inmates or more Families
> than one in one Cottage or House.

Parish officers administering the Act and not fulfilling their duties were subject to heavy fines, and those persons failing to pay the poor rate could end up in prison. The idea of the workhouse probably evolved sometime in the seventeenth century from the combination of the requirement to 'set the poor to work', together with the provision of 'Houses of Dwelling for the impotent Poor'. The Webbs noted that by 1815 there were over 4,000 workhouses and poorhouses in England, containing around 100,000 residents.

Further legislation added detail to the statute of 1601. The Settlement Act of 1662, determined that paupers away from their place of settlement, their 'home' parish, should be sent back to that parish in order not to burden other parishes with the cost of their relief. Acts in 1691 and 1697 clarified and refined how 'settlement' was determined.

The Poor Relief Act, 1722, also known as 'Knatchbull's Act', introduced the idea of a *parish* workhouse operating in a similar way to the later union workhouses; any pauper refusing to enter the workhouse would be denied relief. Later Acts addressed the question of bastardy—whether the father's identity had to be declared, and his financial responsibility for the child, as well as how to define the child's settlement.

These and various other statutes became known as the 'Old Poor Laws'. By the late 18th and early 19th centuries, the cost to the local taxpayer of supporting the poor had risen alarmingly, and one of the main reasons for this was perceived to be what was called 'outdoor relief'. Many able-bodied agricultural labourers were unable to earn sufficient money to support themselves and their families, and relief was provided to those workers effectively subsidizing their inadequate wages. Furthermore, the more mouths they had to feed, the greater was the subsidy. In 1795, the parish of Speenhamland in Berkshire introduced a formal structure to administer this; a sliding scale determined the amount of relief due based on the size of the labourers' families and the price of bread. This system, or variants of it, became adopted by many parishes.

Outdoor relief was subject to considerable criticism. There was no incentive for the worker to seek to better his situation by working hard (or even adequately) to improve productivity, and there was a positive disincentive to limit the size of his family since he and they would be fed regardless. The system encouraged labourers to marry and have large families. Equally, there was no benefit to the employer to reward industry by paying more than a minimum wage, since to do so would effectively subsidize his competitor farmers in the same parish by reducing the overall bill for poor relief.

The issues were spelled out explicitly in the report of the parliamentary select committee set up to investigate the problem of Poor Law expenditure in 1817. Spending on the poor had risen from £1.6M in 1776 to £5.1M in 1815, an increase of well over three times. This was twice as fast as population growth.* The report noted that poor relief had the effect of increasing the population—the system stimulated large families—and reducing the impetus on the labouring classes to work hard and improve their lot; poor relief was encouraging and increasing the misery it was supposed to alleviate. The poor were degraded by the need for parochial support, and the community was oppressed by the financial burden which was only going to increase. The report considered different ways

---

* The population censuses of 1801 and 1811 had demonstrated a population increase from 10.9M to 12.6M—15.5%, or around 1.4% per year. Extrapolating that back to 1776, yields an expected increase in the population between 1776 and 1815 of 1.72 times.

of raising extra revenue and rejected all of these for various reasons. It said that many parishes were in a similar situation as Wombridge in Salop, where the value of 'lands, mines and houses', even if rent free, was insufficient to maintain the poor rate.

The committee considered methods for increasing the rate levied and reducing expenditure, noting at length the excessive legal and other costs associated with settlement issues. A number of suggestions were made; more workhouses and schools for poor children were commended, as well as a change to the way select vestries were appointed. The report finished:

> Conceiving that the House [of Commons] expected at [our] hands a general revision of the whole system of our Poor Laws ... yet the task of providing practical remedies is so arduous ... that even more time and labour would not have been misspent in considering ... numerous proposals ... from different quarters

The House would not, the report continued, be asked to adopt any of the proposals until adequate consultation had taken place.

One item that was acted upon quite soon however, was the question of select vestries whose reputation was by now severely tarnished. A position in a select vestry had been regarded for some time as a self-appointed sinecure for the privileged. In *The Vestry laid Open* by Joseph Phipps, published in 1739, Daniel Defoe was quoted as saying: 'There is not a greater abuse in the world, than that of Select Vestries; it is the most flagrant of tyrannies'. Phipps reported a lawyer's view: 'there is no Act of Parliament which directs a Select Set of Vestry-Men, or particular Vestry-Justices'. The position of parish officer was thought originally to be one of 'expense and trouble', to be performed as a public service. Now, the position was one of 'profit and pleasure'. In 1806, Thomas Rowlandson published a cartoon entitled *A Select Vestry* in which a number of well-fed elderly men in a vestry are drinking large quantities of wine; one seems to be urinating in the corner. The churchwardens, as listed on the wall, have names like *Guttle, Winebibber, and Pinchpoor*. A beadle is angrily using a cane and his foot to keep several thin and ragged paupers, a woman and some children from the workhouse, from coming into the room.

Two Acts relating to the regulation of select vestries followed in 1818 and 1819; the rules for appointing a select vestry were very clearly laid down, together with its wide-ranging duties in respect of administering the Poor Laws, keeping of records, and employing salaried persons to act as overseers of the poor. The major issue, what to do about outdoor relief, was addressed by another select committee which reported in 1824.

This committee was to 'inquire into the practice which prevails in some parts of our country, of paying the Wages of Labour out of the Poor Rates'. It noted the 'vicious' effect of outdoor relief, where it became a matter of indifference to the labourer how hard he worked, since his family would be supported either way. Frequently, the report said, 'the work of four or five such labourers ... might easily be performed by a single labourer'. It noted that persons not in need of farm labour were, via the poor rate, nevertheless required to contribute to their payment. The question of the 'encouragement' of surplus population was addressed; one witness reported labourers threatening to marry in order to gain maintenance. The character of the labouring classes was degraded by the system, and this resulted in perpetual quarrels with the employers. The objective should be to separate the wages of employed labourers from those persons supported by the Poor Rate.

From the evidence presented, it seemed that the problem of subsidizing wages from the Poor Rate was more prevalent in the southern counties—Suffolk, Sussex, Bedfordshire, Buckinghamshire, Dorset, and Wiltshire were noted particularly. It was also observed that magistrates could always refuse to accept Poor Law accounts in an attempt to control expenditure, although the resulting appeals to Quarter Sessions resulted in the further expenditure of time and money. The committee commented that the original Elizabethan Act required the children of paupers to be put to work—it had never been intended that children should be subsidized in the way that was happening, although the committee was against forbidding this by statute.

Recommendations were limited to improving management of the process by using select vestries with salaried overseers, taking account of the character and conduct of the poor to whom relief is given, and proposing the appointment of an inspector of parish Poor Law accounts reporting to a magistrate. Just like the select committee on Poor Law expenditure, the committee identified the problem quite clearly, but were unable to suggest a clear way to solve it.

One other factor in the context of reform needs to be considered. In 1798, an obscure curate from Surrey, Thomas Malthus, published a work that was to be extensively revised and expanded over the next twenty-five years or so. In *An Essay on the Principle of Population*, he sought to apply mathematics, which he had studied at Cambridge, to the issue of population increase and food supply. His contention was that whereas population increases in geometric ratio, one, two, four, eight etc., food supply increases only in arithmetic ratio, one, two, three, four, thus 'population is kept in balance with the food supply by various "checks"'. These checks included war, famine and pestilence, and 'restraint'—delayed marriage, contraception, and prostitution. He gave 'vivid descriptions of the ... consequences of overpopulation and of the brutal means by which populations are checked'. He thus argued against the Poor Laws, since by providing the poor with food the 'natural checks' were negated; he denied that the poor have a right to be supported. In Darwinian terms, he might have said that the provision of relief to the poor reversed Natural Selection. Malthus contended that the laws tended to 'increase the price of food' and to 'undermine the spirit of independence of the people'. The Poor Law encouraged 'early and improvident marriages', creating the poor that were to be maintained.

Although Darwin 'acknowledged Malthus' influence in the theory of natural selection', others called him a 'mischievous booby', 'a precious philosophicide', and 'barbarous and impious'. Nevertheless, the *Oxford Dictionary of National Biography* comments: 'the principle of population became accepted as a central tenet of classical political economy'.

In 1830, grievances among farm labourers on account of their starvation wages boiled over into a full-scale revolt in the southern counties. Threatening letters signed by 'Captain Swing' were sent to farmers and landowners; there were riots and robberies, burglary and theft. Threshing machines and other agricultural machinery were destroyed and ricks and farm buildings were burned down. The rioters were dealt with severely; ten were executed and hundreds were transported to Australia.

Two years later, the reforming Whig government of Earl Grey established a Royal Commission to conduct 'an elaborate investigation' into the Poor Laws. There were nine commissioners, the principal two being the academic Nassau W Senior, and Edwin Chadwick, who had been Jeremy Bentham's private secretary.* The report, published in 1834, and authored mainly by Chadwick, contained nearly 400 pages; a further 8,000 pages of evidence, contained in thirteen appendices, took several more years before it saw the light of day. The main conclusions were expected, and largely uncontroversial:

---

* Jeremy Bentham was the philosopher and social reformer who founded the principle of Utilitarianism.

- Relief to able-bodied persons except within the workhouse should be, henceforth, made illegal; in other words 'outdoor relief', except in special circumstances, should be abolished.

- A central board for administrating the new law should be set up.

- Individual parishes should be grouped into unions with a shared workhouse.

The conclusions were drafted into a bill, 'The Poor Law Amendment Act', which received the Royal Assent on 14 August of the same year. The changes were far-reaching. Under the old system, the Poor Law had been administered locally by parish officers. It was overseen by county magistrates in the more than 15,000 parishes in England and Wales, without any central control. The new Act required the setting up of a Poor Law Commission. Three commissioners, and up to nine assistant commissioners were appointed to oversee the new law; the commissioners reported annually to one of the 'Principal Secretaries of State'. The new 'Union' workhouses would be overseen by a Board of Guardians, and administered by paid officers. The Poor Law Commissioners would be the final arbiters on rules and regulations, previously the province of magistrates.

Mr Duke had qualified as a magistrate in 1816, so for eighteen years he and his fellow magistrates had been the final arbiters in deciding who among the poor was to receive what relief and under what circumstances. Now, that authority had been removed; he was required to act as part of a team— the guardians of the Amesbury Union—and within the terms of the new law. Furthermore, it was now the Poor Law Commissioners who decided on the interpretation of the new legislation. It seems likely that the reduction in Mr Duke's status—as he saw it—and his inability to act according to his own lights in an unconstrained and patrician manner towards the poor, contributed to his increasingly fractious behaviour with his fellow guardians and the commissioners.

The new Act had passed into law but it was not without its dissenters, and one person in particular possessed the resource to broadcast his dissatisfaction to the nation. John Walter, MP for Berkshire, was owner of *The Times*, and prompted by a 'genuine though sentimental humanity', strongly resisted the withdrawal of outdoor relief. The suppression of this relief was to blight the new law, because although the union workhouses would provide universal support for the young, old, destitute, and infirm, this relief was only available *within* the workhouse. As noted previously, to some the idea of entering the workhouse at all was anathema—a humiliation and disgrace not to be endured. Charles Dickens illustrated this attitude in the character of old Betty Higden in *Our Mutual Friend*. She had a horror of being sent to the workhouse and dying there, and kept the money to pay for her funeral hidden in her clothes, preferring to die in the fields.

The editor of *The Times*, Thomas Barnes, ensured that the perceived iniquity of the new law was continuously paraded before his readers, by reporting on inquests into people dying of want where outdoor relief had been refused. Furthermore, the newspaper reported at length and in detail cases of neglect, cruelty, and brutality in workhouses when these came to court, or, as in the Andover case, where a public enquiry ensued. It is interesting to speculate what the effect of publicity on the Amesbury affair might have been, had a reporter from *The Times* been present.

Thomas Barnes was passionately in favour of outdoor relief, but what is notable is that in none of the 110 articles of the new Act was there a specific ordinance abolishing it for the able-bodied or, indeed, mandating the use of unions. The details were left to the commissioners to decide. Article 26 of the Act says: 'it shall be lawful ... to declare so many parishes as they [the commissioners] think fit to be united'. And Article 52:

> And whereas a practice has obtained of giving relief to persons or their families who ... were ... in the employment of individuals, and the relief of the able-bodied and their families is in many places administered in modes productive of evil in other respects: and whereas difficulty may arise in case any immediate and universal remedy is attempted ... that it shall be lawful for the commissioners by such rules ... to declare to what extent and for what period the relief to be given to able bodied persons ... may be administered out of the workhouse.

The commissioners were given considerable flexibility in the determination and application of the new rules. There would have to be a transition period of several years to allow new unions to be established, and a considerable number of new workhouses to be built. But so much publicity had been given to the Commission and the following Act, that the Poor Law Commissioners were keen to ensure that there was no confusion in the minds of the parish officers who had to administer the new law. At the Marlborough Quarter Sessions of October 1834, when Mr Duke was present, a letter from the commissioners was read out. From the *Devizes and Wiltshire Gazette*:

> They [the commissioners] had been led to believe that the overseers of many parishes had been impressed with an idea that they were already exonerated from administering outdoor relief, according to the 43rd of Elizabeth.[*] This was an error ... the commissioners trusted the magistrates would take every opportunity to remove it.

A week later, the newspaper further clarified the situation, possibly at the request of some of the magistrates:

---

[*] The '43rd of Elizabeth' was the 1601 Act, passed in the 43rd year of Queen Elizabeth's reign.

It is feared that many erroneous opinions prevail amongst overseers and others invested with the administration of the [new] Poor Laws ... particularly in relation to the powers of Magistrates in ordering parochial relief—we think it necessary ... to point out that [certain] Acts are not repealed; and that these Acts authorise any Justice of the Peace (except where there is a Board of Guardians, Select Vestry or other similar body, when the mode of relief is left entirely in their hands), on the oath of a pauper, that he has reasonable cause for relief ... and has been refused, to summon two overseers before him to shew cause why relief should not be granted ... to make an order ... or otherwise relieve the able-bodied.

The situation was, therefore, far from clear. The Poor Law Commissioners were in charge and made the rules, but magistrates still had discretionary executive power under certain circumstances. Here was another explanation for Mr Duke's flurry of correspondence with the new commissioners, as he sought guidance on the interpretation of the new law.

## *Appendix 2*
### *The Amesbury Union*

| Parish | Pop. | Area (acres) | Av. Poor exp. (£) 1833 - 1835 | Guardians 1835 |
|---|---|---|---|---|
| Figheldean | 531 | 5,150 | 368 | Mr Hayward |
| Milston | 107 | 1,480 | 75 | Mr Rendall |
| Durrington | 467 | 2,830 | 361 | Mr Rowden |
| Bulford | 290 | 4,160 | 172 | Mr Long Jnr |
| Amesbury | 944 | 6,060 | 581 | Mr Long & Mr Pinckney |
| Durnford | 481 | 3,770 | 388 | Mr Smith |
| Wilsford-cum-Lake | 119 | 1,460 | 52 | Mr Grey |
| Woodford | 397 | 2,280 | 340 | Mr Hughes |
| Maddington | 381 | 4,180 | 242 | Mr Baker |
| Shrewton | 491 | 2,220 | 312 | Mr Charles Wansborough |
| Orcheston St George | 219 | 2,160 | 51 | Mr Mills |
| Orcheston St Mary | 134 | 2,150 | 94 | Mr R Cook |
| Rollstone | 39 | 910 | 60 | Mr Atkins |
| Winterbourne Stoke | 272 | 3,540 | 169 | Mr Burrough |
| Tilshead | 465 | 3,990 | 244 | Mr R Giddings |
| Cholderton | 161 | 1,390 | 74 | Mr P Humphries |
| Newton Toney | 268 | 2,770 | 172 | Mr Judd |
| Boscombe | 80 | 2,000 | 65 | Mr Waters |
| Allington | 148 | 460 | 132 | Mr Horne |
| Idmiston | 520 | 6,160 | 196 | Mr Charles Black |
| Winterbourne Dauntsey | 161 | 1,280 | 82 | Mr Blatch |
| Winterbourne Gunner | 243 | 1,430 | 163 | Mr Job Sutton |
| Winterbourne Earls | 166 | 1,760 | 52 | Mr P Cusse |
| **Totals** | **7,084** | **63,590** | **4,445** | |

It is possible to draw some conclusions about the existing, pre-1834, poor relief in the area by reference to a grid Colonel a'Court attached to his letter, which is reproduced here. The Amesbury Union consisted of twenty-three parishes occupied by 7,084 persons (from the 1831 census); the area was around 100 square miles. The average poor rate levied for the previous three years was £4,445. It is illuminating to examine the criteria that qualified the working poor for relief and the amount that was granted. Relief was applied when the individual's normal weekly wages fell below a certain minimum level. For most parishes this was seven shillings, however three of the parishes used six shillings as the minimum, while another three used eight. A few examples: the parish of Figheldean, population 531, area 368 acres, average annual poor relief for the previous three years £368, set six shillings per week as the minimum below which relief was granted. That relief was a gallon loaf of bread and 3d (three old pence) per head for a man, his wife and each of three children. In April 1836, a gallon loaf of bread cost 10d and wheat was selling at 5.68 shillings per bushel. When a'Court wrote his letter, wheat cost 4.37 shillings per bushel so assuming that the cost of bread scaled approximately with wheat costs, a loaf could be expected to have cost around seven pence, three farthings* or 7¾d. In terms of weekly cost, the relief amounted to 1s 3d plus five loaves at a cost of 3s 2¾d, a total to the parish of 4s 5¾d. The parish of Milston, population 107, granted the same allowance, but the threshold for relief was eight shillings per week, significantly more generous. The parish of Durnford set the threshold at seven shillings per week, but the allowance was a loaf plus 6d for the man, a loaf plus 4d for the woman, and a loaf each for three children, total 10d plus 3s 2¾d worth of bread or 4s ¾d. It is easy to see why this was starvation wages remembering Cobbett's view that

---

\* There were four farthings (1/4d) to one old penny (1d), 12 old pennies to one shilling (1s) and 20 shillings to one pound Sterling (£1).

three times as much was a reasonable amount just for food. A 'gallon' loaf of bread was made with a gallon of flour and weighed 8lbs 11oz or 8.7lbs.* A man doing eight to ten hours manual labour needs around 3000 calories—approximately 1100 calories being provided by 1lb of bread. No work was done on Sunday, but it was still necessary to eat—say seventy per cent of a working day—so a simple calculation shows that a working man alone needs around 18.3 lbs of bread per week just for subsistence.† Of course if the man was out of work he would need to eat significantly less, nevertheless if he was working but his wages were below the threshold, his bread requirements corresponded to around 40% of the value of the relief. Everything else, food for the wife and three children, clothes, heating, and rent, was expected to be purchased out of the remainder plus whatever wages—less than seven shillings—was left. The average cost to the parish of 'outdoor' relief for a family of five can be computed to be around 5s per week, equivalent to £13 per year, or £2 12s per head per annum.

If the new workhouse, designed to hold 150 paupers, was entirely filled with working men and their families previously in receipt of outdoor relief, that would equate to a cost of said relief of only £390, less than ten per cent of the annual average relief bill of £4,445 for the Amesbury Union. In fact, a significant number of workhouse inmates would be orphans, the aged, and the infirm, so the previous cost of outdoor relief must have been significantly less than £390, and the far more significant burden of the poor on the parish was comprised of those really incapable of supporting themselves, i.e. parentless children, those too old to work, and those unable to work due to accident, disease or other disablement. There were other costs relating to the poor. The mothers of bastard children

---

\*   1lb = one pound weight, 1oz = one ounce weight, 16oz = 1lb, 2.25lb = 1Kg.

†   A diet of bread alone would have been intolerable. Some butter, cheese, vegetables, and occasionally meat, would also have to be purchased.

were allowed a similar amount to that for labouring men and there was also support for looking after the poor in infirmaries. A proposal of £35 was subsequently made by the Board of Guardians of the Amesbury Union for this purpose, and this was probably in line with what had been paid previously. There had also been salaries for the parish officers and other expenses, a significant one being that related to legal costs in the case of contested settlement. A substantial expense following the new Act, would be the cost of building a union workhouse; the government provided the loan which had to be repaid out of the poor rate. The initial cost of the Amesbury workhouse was £3,500.

## *Appendix 3*

*Mr Duke's 1842 list of complaints and comments from the PLC on the main ones following Parker's enquiry.*

1. That for want of a proper hospital a man was suffered to die in the old men's board of the dropsy and other old men in health were permitted to occupy the same room day and night whilst maggots were dropping from the putrefied wounds of the dying man, the room being kept constantly sprinkled with vinegar and chlorate of lime, and the master for his self-defence entering in with a ladle of pitch in the one hand and a red hot poker in the other wherewith to keep it constantly stirred.

2. To keeping in lodging at Salisbury Jane Conduit and her four children under the allowance of four 4lb loaves and one and nine in money she being at the last stage apparently of existence having 2/3d to pay weekly for lodging and leaving her only one shilling per week with four loaves for the maintenance of herself and four children—refusing to remove this family to the union house on the urgent representation of Mr Duke and thus obliging him to remove the woman for the purpose of saving her life, on his own responsibility—the woman having at the time of her removal gradually placed in pawn for the sake of sustenance, all her clothes with the exception of the shift and night gown she then had on, and her testament—all the articles pawned were redeemed for her by Mr Duke who was arraigned by the union for this necessary act of humanity and wrongly censored by Mr Hughes the vice-chairman.

3. The making of partial decisions on the grocery tenders so much so as to cause one of the competitors for the time to withdraw.

4.  The union of the Chairman and Clerk in the illegal ejection of the occupants of some cottages at Maddington sold under the Poor Law Act ... the clerk acting as the advising attorney of the purchasers, and the chairman sanctioning this illegal ejection by the sending a policeman to keep the peace. In one instance a man was collared, violently propelled from his house and on his ejectment received a bind [?] behind; the assault was compromised by the payment of money to the party injured, the clerk aiding in the arrangement. In another instance the key of the house occupied by a female was obtained by the chairman by a stratagem, the woman locked out, her house forcibly taken possession of, [and] her goods turned out into her garden where the woman remained in the open air the whole of the night. Legal proceedings were about to be taken against the Chairman but were afterwards withdrawn at the intercession of the Rev E Duke.

5.  Dealing at Romsey—24 miles distant for shoes of a man of the name of Roper—an old friend of the master's and sending them to the same place to be cobbled whilst shoemakers in Amesbury would readily make and mend at the same terms.

6.  The dishonourable dismissal of Mrs Wiltshire of Amesbury as Butcher, and employment of Mr Marlowe of Salisbury the Butcher of Mr Wilson the clerk.

7.  The withdrawal of the order cheque book as being useless.

8.  The endeavoured expulsion of Mr Pyle—the surgeon of the Union House, and the endeavoured substitution of Mr Turner—a medical gentleman resident at Shrewton, the neighbouring parish to the chairman who was sent by the latter, the chairman, to Mr Pyle, to inform him that it would be useless for him to tender, for his tender at any sum would not be accepted.

9. The refusal to advertise for tenders for clothing but entering all such orders in the Master's Petty Order book and leaving the master—the servant of the establishment to purchase of whom and where he please.

10. The non-employment of a porter.

11. The collusion against the Reverend E. Duke by the refusal ever to second a motion proceeding from him, and often passing it by even in silence.

12. The want of a proper and weekly supply of garments to the female paupers.

13. Badness of soup—deficiency of meat, improper boiling of peas and badness of gruel.

14. The non-reading of evening prayers to the men.

15. The unnecessary reduction of bread allowance to the outdoor paupers by giving 4lb loaves instead of those of 4 lbs 5½ ounces under the alleged but mistaken obligation of an Act of Parliament.

16. The keeping of no account books of clothing—no inventory.

17. The keeping of no account book of the purchase & sale of pigs.

18. The bad state of the yards—the children in the event of a thaw or wet weather being prevented taking due exercise therein.

19. The noisome state of the privies.

20. The annual election of a vice chairman whose state of health obliges him to be absent through the whole winter season.

21. From the neglect of properly warming the house the inmates suffered most dreadfully during the severe season of 1840-41 and there are now wanting stoves for the chapel and some of the wards—also for the entrance hall on Board days.

22. The irregular admission of paupers on Board days.

23. The non-attendance of the master on the guardians on Board days—the occupation of the committee room by the relieving officers when not on business—the taking of a place at the table by the clerk and his continual interference with every subject discussed at the board out of his ordinary line of duties.

24. The want of vagrant reception rooms.

25. The want of a hearse.

There was also an 'NB': the inconvenience of fortnightly meetings, the bearers of corpses laying out for disposal of the clothes of deceased paupers, and the master's cash book. Mr Duke, himself, subsequently withdrew seven of the charges, nos 1,3,4,6,7,8 & 11.

Henry Walter Parker held a one-day enquiry on these complaints and sent a report to the PLC. Their response is reproduced below:

> The commissioners have attentively examined the evidence upon these charges, and with the exception of the evidence relative to the omission to purchase articles for the supply of the clothing stores by tender, they find nothing to warrant the imputation upon the Board of Guardians and no proof whatever to support the charges impugning the character of individual guardians and the officers of the board. The commissioners understand that Mr Duke himself abandoned the charges 1,3,4,6,7,8 & 11.

The first charge brought under the notice of the Assistant Commissioner, imputes to the Board of Guardians and the officers charged with the management of the workhouse, the disregard of the health of the pauper inmates and raises the inference that the workhouse Master, regardless of the inmates under his care, did not fail to adopt means to preserve his own health. The evidence upon this subject discloses one of those painful cases which are not unfrequently met with in similar establishments. A man of a peculiarly obstinate disposition, resident in a cottage and protected by two fierce dogs, became seriously ill and ultimately bed-ridden, in which state he remained for nine days no person daring to approach him. The circumstances at last became known to the parish authorities, and means were resorted to, to beat off the dogs. The man was then removed to the union workhouse where it was ascertained that his body, from lying on a bed rotten with his own excrement, had become a mass of sores in which maggots had been engendered. His admission into the workhouse in this deplorable condition took place on 22 May 1837 where he was immediately cleansed and placed in a bed specially prepared for his accommodation in the old men's ward. The quantity of water discharged by sores in his legs rendering it expedient to place him in the infirmary wards in the upper part of the building. After the man's removal to the workhouse a marked improvement took place in his health which declined again however in the succeeding winter, and death ensued on 14 December, nearly 7 months after his admission. It appears that towards the close of his days, the sores in his legs and body became so exceedingly offensive as to render it necessary to remove the pauper inmates of the board into other apartments. The inconvenience attending this distribution of the other inmates into other parts of the building pointed out the necessity for providing the hospital wards on the ground floor which were subsequently erected. The statement of the medical officer that the master of the workhouse used every endeavour to prevent any bad consequences from the offensive state of the poor man's sores shows that it was judicious to remove the effluvia by burning pitch and to disinfect the air by sprinkling the room with vinegar and chloride of lime.

With respect to the charge that the clothing stores are not supplied by contract it is admitted that a contrary course has been adopted. The practice of authorising the matron to purchase particular articles however advantageous it may appear and the average cost of the paupers' clothing shows that it has not been attended with loss, opens the door to the private patronage which should not be intrusted to any officer. If this system of tender has not been found to be so beneficial as might have been expected some misapprehension respecting the contracts may have given rise to doubts in the minds of tradespeople and rendered them careless of sending in tenders. To restore confidence with the tradespeople the commissioners recommend that the estimated quantity of articles required for the pauper's clothing should be procured by tender quarterly and the quality of the respective articles to be supplied should accord with samples of the articles now in use.

With respect to the charges more particularly affecting the matron, the Commissioners desire to observe that no regulation issued by them requires a weekly supply of outer garments and that the evidence of the linen having been changed weekly and of the matron's attention to the cleanly appearance of the females gowns shows that the utmost attention has been paid to this subject. The evidence respecting the preparation of the paupers' food shows that all reasonable suggestions upon that subject have been attended to, that the pauper inmate most competent to the duty has been employed in the kitchen and that the inmates testify their satisfaction with the food supply to them.

With respect to the omission to keep the clothing accounts the Commissioners found however that the master has expressed his willingness to receive instructions therein and that the Assistant Commissioner proposes to take an opportunity to explain them to him.

The case of Jane Conduit is one in which Mr Duke appears to have acted under a misapprehension of the state of the law as well as the circumstances of the case, for assuming that Jane Conduit and her children were reduced to the state of distress Mr Duke supposed them to be in, it was the duty of the officers of the parish in which she resided to provide her with medical assistance and relief. The law has humanely provided that in a case such as this was supposed to be, the parish in which the pauper is resident shall provide the relief which may be required and that all questions as to settlement shall be subsequently determined. The commissioners therefore regard Mr Duke's interference in this case as unnecessary [*illegal* was crossed out in the draft copy and replaced by *unnecessary*] and injudicious being contrary to the wise and humane provision which requires the destitute sick to be relieved instantly in the parish in which they fall. But it does not even appear that Mr Duke's impression of the condition of the woman and her family was correct; one of the children supposed to be with her having been previously received into the workhouse and the complaint of the woman differed from that which she was supposed to be labouring under.

Having thus adverted to the most serious charges, the Commissioners do not think it necessary to offer any remarks upon the numerous other charges. Nevertheless they cannot conclude this communication without expressing their regret that a magistrate and a clergyman should adduce charges of so serious a nature as some of these charges undoubtedly are upon insufficient grounds and that when visiting the workhouse he so far forget his duty as to use language calculated to impair its discipline.

[signed] Secretary,

21 May 1842

## Appendix 4
### *George Wheeler's age and details of his family*

There is some uncertainty about George Wheeler's age. Central Registration and the workhouse records give his age at death as seventeen. The parish burial register at Figheldean recorded his age as fifteen. His baptism in the same parish took place on 29 August 1824, so either age could be correct since his date of birth was not recorded; if he was seventeen when he died, more than a year would have elapsed between his birth and baptism which seems unlikely.

Charles Wheeler, George's brother, in the evidence he gave in April 1844, said that he (Charles) was twelve years old 'last Michaelmas Day'. Michaelmas Day falls on 29 September, so if he turned twelve on 29 September 1843, then he was born on 29 September 1831. The parish register at Figheldean records his baptism on 9 October 1831, ten days later.

George Wheeler was frequently described as a 'boy' in the documentation. His three aunts were present at the funeral, and were likely to be more familiar with his age than the workhouse master, who was the informant of the death to Central Registration as well as the workhouse records. The aunts would have probably told the parish clerk the correct age as they understood it, being his close relatives. Furthermore, if George was a similar age to his brother Charles at baptism, it would suggest that his birth fell in August 1824, and his age when he died on 17 April 1840 really was fifteen years as stated in the parish record.

Considering this evidence together, it can be concluded that George Wheeler's probable age at death was fifteen, and not seventeen as stated in Central Registration.

Details of George's immediate family can be assembled from the parish records:

David Wheeler of Figheldean, married Sarah Kill at Netheravon, 29 March 1822.

Sarah died 17 May 1838, of 'decline'; David died 15 April 1839, of consumption.

Children:

Elizabeth, baptised 23 June 1822, buried 20 May 1837

George, baptised 29 August 1824, buried 19 April 1840

Charles, baptised 19 October 1831

Thomas, baptised 7 August 1836, buried 23 July 1837

Mary, baptised 7 August 1836

From the 1851 census, Mary is recorded as aged fourteen, indicating that she and Thomas were twins. Charles is found in the 1861 census, aged twenty-nine, a soldier at Aldershot.

# Bibliography

*Abury, A Temple of the British Druids,* William Stukeley, London, 1743.

*The Ancient History of South Wiltshire,* Sir Richard Colt Hoare, BART, London, William Miller, 1812.

*The Annals of the World,* James Ussher, E Tyler for F Crook, London, 1658.

*The Barrow Diggers,* (Charles Wools), Whittaker & Co, London, 1839.

*The Druidical Temples of the County of Wilts,* Rev E Duke, London, John Russell Smith, 1846.

*Druids, A Very Short Introduction,* B Cunliffe, Oxford University Press, 2010.

*English Criminal Justice in the Nineteenth Century,* Bentley, Hambledon Press, London, 1998.

*English Poor Law History, Part 1: The Old Poor Law,* Sidney and Beatrice Webb, English Local Government, Volume 7, Frank Cass, London, 1963.

*An Essay on the Principle of Population,* Thomas Malthus, London, 1798.

*From Antiquary to Archaeologist,* biography of William Cunnington, Robert Cunnington, Ed James Dyer, Shire Publications, Princes Risborough, 1975.

*The History of the Telescope,* Henry C King, Charles Griffin & Co Ltd, High Wycombe, 1955.

*Letter to the Right Hon. Sir James Graham Bart on the ... Andover Union,* Henry Walker Parker, Simkin Marshall & Co, London, 1845.

*Matryona's House,* Alexander Solzhenitsyn, Translated by Michael Glenny, Bodley Head, 1970.

*Middlemarch,* George Eliot, Blackwood, Edinburgh and London, 1872.

*Oxford Dictionary of National Biography,* Oxford University Press, online.

*Oxford English Dictionary,* Oxford University Press, online.

*The Parochial History of Bremhill ...,* W L Bowles, John Murray, London, 1828.

*Phillimore Atlas and Index of Parish Registers,* 3rd edition, ed. C R Humphery-Smith, Phillimore, 2010

*Plain Remarks upon the New Poor Law Amendment Act more particularly addressed to the Labouring Classes,* Thomas Garnier, Jacob & Johnson, Winchester, 1835.

*Prolusiones Historicae Illustrative of The Halle of John Halle,* Vol 1, Rev Edward Duke, Brodie, Salisbury, 1837.

*Recreations in Astronomy,* Lewis Tomlinson, John W. Parker, London, 1840.

*Rural Rides,* William Cobbett, published by William Cobbett, London, 1830.

*Stonehenge and Abury, An Illustration of ...* H Browne, Salisbury, Printed by Brodie and Dowding, 1823.

*The Scandal of the Andover Workhouse,* Anstruther, Geoffrey Bles, London, 1973.

*Stonehenge, A Temple restored to the British Druids,* 1740, William Stukeley.

*A Tour in Quest of Genealogy,* 'A Barrister', (Richard Fenton), Sherwood, Neely and Jones, London, 1811.

*The Vestry laid Open,* Joseph Phipps, Millan and Noble, London, 1739.

*Wiltshire Worthies,* Stratford, Brown & Co, London, 1882.

www.workhouses.org.uk, Peter Higginbotham.

# References

*An Act for the Amendment and better Administration of the Laws relating to the Poor in England and Wales,* 4 & 5 Gulielmi IV, Cap 75 & 76, 1834.

*An Act for the Relief of the Poor,* 43 Eliz., Cap 2, 1603.

Amesbury Union correspondence with the Poor Law Commissioners, 1839 - 1842, MH12/13659; 1843 - 1846, MH12/ 13660, National Archives.

*Annual Report of the Poor Law Commissioners,* Charles Knight, London, 1835.

The *Chadwick Papers,* UCL, Special Collections.

The *Christian Remembrancer,* a Quarterly Review, Vol XII, July – December 1846, PP 467 – 477.

Minutes, Amesbury Union, 1835 - 1839, H2/110/1; 1845 - 1894, H2/110/4-11, Wiltshire & Swindon History Centre.

*Poor Law Commissioners' Report,* 1834, (copy), London, 1905.

*Report from the Select Committee on the Poor Laws,* House of Commons, London, 1817.

*Report from the Select Committee on Labourers Wages,* House of Commons, London, 1824.

Transcript of Correspondence between Cunnington and Colt Hoare, Wiltshire Museum, Devizes, unpublished.


## Newspapers and Journals

*Devizes and Wiltshire Gazette*

*Exeter Gazette*

*Gentleman's Magazine,* between 1813 and 1849

*Hull Packet*

*John Bull*

*Proceedings of the Linnean Society*

*Literary Gazette*
*London Courier and Evening Gazette*
*Metropolitan Magazine*
*Monthly Review*
*Morning Chronicle*
*Salisbury and Wiltshire Herald*
*Salisbury and Winchester Journal*
*Salisbury Herald*
*Salisbury Journal*
*South Australian Register*
*The Spectator*
*The Sun*
*The Times*
*Wiltshire Notes and Queries,* March 1915, et seq.

# Picture credits

*Fig 1.* Portrait of Edward Duke, by kind permission of the British Library.

*Fig 2.* Watercolour of Lake House, by kind permission of the Wiltshire Museum and Archive and Library © Wiltshire Museum, Devizes.

*Fig 3.* Edward Duke's family tree, drawn by the author.

*Fig 4.* Edward Duke's planetarium, drawn by the author.*

*Fig 5.* Detail of the planetarium elements, drawn by the author.*

*Fig 6.* Photograph of the Amesbury Union Workhouse, by kind permission of Wiltshire and Swindon Archives, Geoffrey Crowe Collection.

*Fig 7.* Layout of the Amesbury Union Workhouse from the 25 inch Ordnance Survey map.*

*Fig 8.* Locations in the narrative, from the 6 inch Ordnance Survey map, drawn by the author.*

*Front and back cover:* Amesbury from the 25 inch Ordnance Survey map,* Edward Duke—per *Fig 1*, and the Amesbury Workhouse, by kind permission of the Charlotteville Jubilee Trust.

* Extracts from the 1890s Ordnance Survey 6 inch and 25 inch maps reproduced under a Creative Commons Attribution-NonCommercial-ShareAlike 4.0 International (CC-BY-NC-SA) licence with the permission of the National Library of Scotland.

# Index

## C

# G

# H

# I

# J

# K

# L

## M

## N